"Dr. Wesley's commitment to scholarship, ministry, and the Word of our God is impeccable. As with previous literary works of Dr. Wesley, *A Study of Ephesians* enthusiastically engages the reader with a brilliant exegesis and expression of Scripture. This book is a testament to Dr. Wesley's unique gift to make an ancient text speak to a postmodern world in creative and dynamic ways."

—Dr. R. Timothy Jones, Peaceful Rest Baptist Church
Shreveport, Louisiana

"Dr. Wesley's book makes easier the understanding of fundamental Bible doctrine through masterful alliteration, accurate interpretation, and creative application. His clarity, command of facts, and concern for contextual integrity will enlighten, encourage, and empower disciples of Jesus Christ to 'rightly divide the Word of truth.'"

—Pastor Eddie L. Jenkins, Good Street Baptist Church
Dallas, Texas

"*A must read!* Dr. Wesley has captured the essence of the book of Ephesians in a riveting and inspiring expose. It is enormously encouraging to believers to follow Christ and work together in love and unity, even in the midst of trials. This is a practical guide believers can use to enhance their relationship with Christ!"

—Dr. Reginald Woullard, Shady Grove Baptist Church
Hattiesburg, Mississippi

A STUDY OF THE BOOK OF
EPHESIANS
THE ROAD TO REDEMPTION AND RECONCILIATION

DR. KARRY D. WESLEY

REDEMPTION
PRESS

Published by Redemption Press, PO Box 427, Enumclaw, WA 98022. Toll Free (844) 2REDEEM (273-3336)

Redemption Press is honored to present this title in partnership with the author. The views expressed or implied in this work are those of the author. Redemption Press provides our imprint seal representing design excellence, creative content, and high quality production.

All Bible quotations are taken from the *King James Version* of the Bible.

ISBN 13: 978-1-68314-022-1 (Print)
          978-1-68314-023-8 (ePub)
          978-1-68314-024-5 (Mobi)

Library of Congress Catalog Card Number: 2016944593

DEDICATION

I WOULD LIKE to dedicate this book to my wife, Cheryl, and my three sons: Christopher (Skylan), Karl (Jasmine), and Charles. They have always been a source of inspiration for me. Then there are my first grandchildren, Kamden James and Karter Monea Wesley. I probably could have finished writing this book several months ago but when they were around, Papa had to turn off the computer to hang out with them (I enjoyed it every time).

I would also like to dedicate this book to the staff of the Antioch Fellowship Church in Dallas. Their commitment to ministry has always allowed me to focus on teaching and preaching. As a result of their hard work, I can spend time writing books like this one to bless the church.

Finally, I would like to dedicate this book to a couple of members of the Antioch Fellowship Church by the names of James and Bessie Bailey. Brother Bailey served as the chairman of the Deacon Ministry for over twenty years. Both of them authenticate what it means to be servants of the Lord. They love God and demonstrate it by loving God's people.

CONTENTS

INTRODUCTION

THIS LETTER TO the Christians in Ephesus was written by Paul while imprisoned in Rome. Most scholars believe it was written between AD 60-63. Since it was written from prison, it is often called one of "the prison epistles," along with the letters written to the Philippians, Colossians, and to Philemon. In this book, you will notice me using several references to scriptures from the book of Colossians. This is intentional because the letters written to the Christians in Ephesus and Colossae are almost identical in content.

Redemption and reconciliation are the primary themes of the book of Ephesians. Paul places emphasis on Jesus "bridging" the gap between man and God. He shows how the death, burial, and resurrection of Jesus Christ open the door for all to be saved, including the Gentiles. Jesus Christ removed the wall between the Gentiles and Jews.

As we shall see in this study, Paul spends a lot of time addressing the doctrinal position of believers before focusing on the practical duties. In Ephesians 1-3, you will notice that he shares a lot of the same doctrinal information over and over again. This is intentional. If Christians don't have the right doctrinal beliefs, the practical behavior will be out of order. On the other hand, when the doctrine is right, the practice will be righteous.

As you read through this material that I have compiled, it is my prayer that you will be informed and inspired. The material in this book is not designed to be a deep theological discourse on Paul's letter to the Ephesians. In most of my writings, I try to use the homiletical approach to give the reader a basic understanding of the material. I believe this approach will at least create a hunger and thirst for the reader to continue studying and learning more from God's Word.

Chapter 1

THE SPIRITUAL BLESSINGS FOR GOD'S FAMILY

EPHESIANS 1:1-7

The Genesis of the Church
The Prisoner Communicating
The Previous Contact
The Planted Church
The Participants' Comprehension
The Partial Conversion
The Presented Christ
The Power Confirmed
The Process Completed
The Preaching Continued

The Greetings to the Church
The Assembly Gathered
The Ascribed Generalization
The Anchored Group

The Attainable Goal
The Amazing Grace
The Additional Gift
The Almighty God

The Gifts for the Church
The Blessed Recipients
The Birth Registry
The Blameless Results
The Blemishes Removed
The Blended Relationship
The Blood Ransom
The Bound Released
The Bridge Reopened

SALVATION IS THE greatest blessing we have received. If you are financially bankrupt but saved, you are blessed. If you are physically sick but saved, you are blessed. In the opening chapter, Paul deals with the spiritual blessings that we have received in Jesus Christ.

THE GENESIS OF THE CHURCH

It is important to know that Paul is **the prisoner communicating** to the Christians in Ephesus. In the book of Ephesians, Paul is communicating to the church by letter because he is imprisoned in Rome at the time this letter is written. It is one of the four "prison epistles" written by Paul when he was under house arrest at Rome. Before dealing with Ephesians, I needed to look at another passage to show Paul's connection to the believers in Ephesus. As a matter of fact, turn to Acts 19 for a few minutes.

Although Paul is writing the letter to the Ephesians from prison, **the previous contact** should be mentioned before we continue. This is not a letter designed to introduce himself to the Christians in Ephesus. Paul had spent time in Ephesus before being imprisoned in Rome. According to Acts 19:1, he arrived in Ephesus and found certain disciples. According to Acts 19:7, there were twelve disciples in Ephesus at the time. These twelve disciples started believing in Jesus as a result of the preaching of Apollos.

It is believed by many theologians that **the planted church** was an act of Paul rather than Apollos. How could Paul be credited for planting this church if when he arrived there were disciples there? Apollos had been there before Paul arrived but the Ephesus church had not been officially established. As we shall see in just a moment, the preaching of Apollos had led to repentance and not reconciliation. Apollos had started the process but God sent Paul to complete it.

It is true that they were called disciples but the truth is that **the participants' comprehension** did not line up with a true understanding of the gospel message. As disciples, they had some knowledge of Jesus but they didn't really know Him by way of the Holy Spirit.

In Acts 19:2, Paul asked the twelve disciples, "Have ye received the Holy Ghost since you believed?" The Greek translation is like this: "Did you receive the Holy Ghost when you believed?" For many, this sounds strange. How could they be called disciples without knowing about the Holy Ghost? Some would even take this passage to mean that you become saved first and then you receive the Holy Ghost later. Apollos had ministered to this group but had not shared the whole counsel of God. He was a powerful orator but he needed to grow and become more knowledgeable of the whole truth (see Acts 18:24-26).

Paul had to address **the partial conversion** of the disciples. The word *conversion* basically means "to be changed." Conversion involves the three Rs (*recognizing* your sins, *repenting* from sin, and *receiving* the Savior). They had only made it to Step 2. When they expressed to Paul that they didn't have a clue as to what he was talking about, Paul knew he had to dig a little deeper into their conversion experience. He wanted to know unto what they were baptized (see Acts 19:2-3). They responded by saying, "John's baptism." Paul had to explain John's baptism to them. He said, "John verily baptized with the baptism of repentance saying unto the people that they should believe on him which should come after him, that is, on Christ Jesus" (Acts 19:4). Paul did not degrade their incomplete faith. Neither did he rebuke them. He took time to explain it to them.

As a result of their response, we have **the presented Christ**. Basically, Paul explained that John the Baptist served as the forerunner of Jesus Christ to prepare the way for Him. After repentance, it was absolutely necessary for them to receive Jesus Christ as their Lord and Savior. After he presented Christ to them, they were baptized in the name of Jesus (see Acts 19:5). The work performed by Apollos made Paul's assignment a whole lot easier. In a real sense, the twelve disciples were ripe for picking because the ministry of Apollos prepared them for the next phase.

In Acts 19:6, we have **the power confirmed** after Paul lays his hands on them. Paul laid hands on them and the Holy Ghost came on them, and they spake with tongues and prophesied (see Acts 19:6). The passage does not say that Paul laid hands on them so they could receive the Holy Spirit. The text tells us that he laid hands and God's Spirit came on them. The image is powerful here. The new converts witnessed proof of their salvation immediately. God allowed them to receive confirmation of their salvation by allowing an outward manifestation of the inward metamorphosis that occurred in their lives.

As a result of Apollos and Paul, we see **the process completed** for the twelve disciples. The process of genuine conversion took place in their lives. The disciples were saved, sanctified, and filled with the Holy Spirit. Now the church has been planted in Ephesus and the work of ministry is activated. God used Apollos and Paul to touch the lives of the people in Ephesus. Please know that the point of this section is not to paint a picture of one person being better than the other. I agree that God used Paul to plant the church, but the work of Apollos was just as valuable. In 1 Corinthians 3:6-7, Paul said, "I have planted, Apollos watered; but God gave the increase. So then neither is he that planteth any thing, neither he that watereth; but God that giveth the increase." Therefore, it is not about Apollos or Paul but God's miraculous work.

In Acts 19:8, we are told that **the preaching continued** in Ephesus after this powerful conversion experience. Paul continued preaching for three months in the temple until the Jews stirred up trouble. He moved the disciples to the School of Tyrannus and continued preaching and teaching for another two years before departing. Paul was constantly under attack during this five-month span but he continued to preach and teach the Word of God. Just before his departure, we are told "So mightily grew the word of God and prevailed" (Acts 19:20). In other words,

the people starting growing spiritually before Paul was led by
the Spirit to leave.

THE GREETINGS TO THE CHURCH

Now let's go back to the book of Ephesians and picture **the
assembly gathered** after receiving this letter from Paul. During the
early days of Christianity, the believers didn't have a bound Bible
with this letter in it. They couldn't turn to the book of Ephesians
and read the first chapter. They didn't have a Bible app on their
iPad to click on. They would assemble together and have the
letters from Paul, Peter, John, James, and others read aloud.

Let's deal with **the ascribed generalization** of the assembly. The
letter is written to "the saints which are at Ephesus, and to the
faithful in Christ Jesus" (Ephesians 1:1). All of the believers were
connected. It was the cross of Calvary that linked them together.
Notice that the letter was written to the "saints" which were at
Ephesus. Yes, they are called saints. Which of the believers in the
assembly are saints? All of them fit this category. The term *saint*
is believed by many to represent the ultimate state or highest
level of spirituality. In actuality, it is really a generalization
representing all believers.

The term does not refer to a few people with great spiritual
qualities. The word *saint* means set apart, consecrated, and holy.
The saint is a follower of Jesus who has been set apart to live for
God. Yes, the saint has been set apart to live for God but this
does not mean he is doing it. In Colossians 3:10, Paul said, "And
have put on the new man, which is renewed in knowledge after
the image of him that created him." The new man has been put
on but this does not necessarily mean he is acting new. The same
is true for what he says in 2 Corinthians 5:17, "Therefore if any
man be in Christ, he is a new creature: old things are passed
away; behold, all things are become new."

I believe the second description in Ephesians 1:1 represents **the anchored group** in Christ. Paul describes them as "the faithful in Christ Jesus." It is great to be a saint but better to be a saint who is faithful in Christ Jesus. The faithful one is not just someone who has placed his faith in Jesus but he has also chosen to totally commit his life to Christ. In Matthew 12:50, Jesus said, "For whosoever shall do the will of my Father which is in heaven, the same is my brother, and sister, and mother." In 1 John 2:17, John says, "And the world passeth away, and the lust thereof: but he that doeth the will of God abideth forever." The psalmist said, "I delight to do thy will, O my God: yea, thy law is within my heart" (Psalm 40:8). The term *faithful* is used as both a noun and an adjective. As a noun, the faithful are those who have placed their faith in Jesus. As an adjective, you are dealing with the faithful saints who are committed to doing things according to the Lord's command.

We should view faithfulness as **the attainable goal** for all believers. When there are faithful in the midst, it shows us that the status is reachable. In other words, if you can be anchored in Christ, so can I. Faithfulness is an attainable goal that simply requires a sincere commitment from the believer. It is great when a person accepts Jesus Christ as his Savior. The believer does absolutely nothing on his own to be saved. Jesus Christ did it all. However, Jesus desires to become Savior and Lord. He is Lord when we sincerely submit to His orders and abide by His words.

In all of the Pauline epistles, Paul always places emphasis on **the amazing grace** we have received as believers. Here he says, "Grace be to you" (Ephesians 1:2a). Paul is not providing grace but reminding them of the grace they had received by being saints. Grace means all the favors from God. It is dealing with the unmerited favor we receive as a result of being a believer. It deals with salvation and all other favors. Later on in Ephesians Paul said, "That in the ages to come he might show the exceeding riches of his grace in his kindness toward us through Christ

Jesus" (Ephesians 2:7). In 2 Corinthians 8:9, Paul said, "For ye know the grace of our Lord Jesus Christ, that, though he was rich, yet for your sakes he became poor, that ye through his poverty might be rich." As if grace were not enough, he comments on **the additional gift** we have received from God. Not only have we received grace, we also have peace (shalom). This is an interesting term that deals with a settled or calm spirit no matter what circumstances exist. In John 14:27, Jesus said, "Peace I leave with you, my peace I give unto you: not as the world giveth, give I unto you. Let not your heart be troubled, neither let it be afraid."

This grace and peace come from **the Almighty God** (see Ephesians 1:2). God is responsible for this grace and peace. He is the only source or provider of grace and peace in the spiritual sense. You can't receive it from any other means. It comes from God the Father through Jesus Christ the Son. It is all-sufficient grace. God gives peace that passes understanding.

THE GIFTS FOR THE CHURCH

As believers, we are **the blessed recipients** from our heavenly Father. Paul said, "Blessed be the God and Father of our Lord Jesus Christ, who hath blessed us with all spiritual blessings in heavenly places in Christ" (Ephesians 1:3). In this passage, God's blessings are spiritual and heavenly, not material blessings. These are not temporal blessings that will one day fade away. These are blessings of the inner man. These spiritual blessings are only found in Jesus Christ.

In **the birth registry** in heaven, the name of every believer is recorded. This registry includes all believers—past, present, and future. This is where the process becomes confusing to people. He has *chosen us* in him before the foundation of the world. In Ephesians 1:5, he says, "Having predestinated us unto the adoption of children by Jesus Christ to himself." Let me deal with four terms that will help us with this series on Ephesians. The terms are *adoption, predestination, foreordained,* and *elect.* God has a birth registry with every person born from Adam to the end of time. Millions and millions of names are recorded in this registry. God has adopted us as children.

It was predestinated, that is, foreordained. The term means "destined before" or "predetermined." Predestination and foreordained simply mean that events and situations in the plan of God are made certain in advance. Let's look briefly at Romans 8:28-29. Paul said, "And we know that all things work together for good to them that love God, to them who are the called according to his purpose. For whom he did foreknow, he also did predestinate to be conformed to the image of his Son, that he might be the firstborn among many brethren." The word does not mean that God chooses some persons for salvation and everyone else for eternal punishment. In eternity past, God chose (elected, predestinated, adopted) some individuals to receive salvation and to be conformed to the image of His Son. He does not force anyone to believe but he knows who will believe.

God is not in heaven wondering whose names will be included in the Lamb's Book of Life. He already knows. It was the pleasure of God and His purpose to adopt us. In John 15:16 Jesus says, "Ye have not chosen me, but I have chosen you, and ordained you, that ye should go and bring forth fruit, and that your fruit should remain: that whatsoever ye shall ask of the Father in my name, he may give it you." In Ephesians 1:5, he says, "Having predestinated us unto the adoption of children by Jesus Christ to himself." Let's spend a few minutes dealing with this action of God.

Look at **the blameless results** that come after being selected by Him. Now let's go back to the end of Ephesians 1:4. He has chosen us " . . . that we should be *holy and without blame* before him in love" (emphasis added)." After being chosen, we become holy and blameless before Him in love. The word *holy (hagious)* means set apart and consecrated just like the word *saint* discussed before. The word *blameless* (*amomous*) means to be free from sin, dirt, and filth. In Philippians 2:15, Paul says, "That ye may be blameless and harmless, the sons of God, without rebuke, in the midst of a crooked and perverse nation, among whom ye shine as lights in the world."

As a result of our selection by God, we have **the blemishes removed** from our lives. This means that the blemishes have been removed because of the divine covering. This means when He comes back for the church, which will be without spot or wrinkle, He will find it even though all of us will still have some sin issues. In 2 Peter 3:14, Peter says, "Wherefore, beloved, seeing that ye look for such things, be diligent that ye may be found of him in peace, without spot and blameless." The believer's perfection is in Christ and Christ alone.

The believer's perfection is due to **the blended relationship** between the saint and the Savior. As a result of being "in Christ" now, the Father does not see us as we are from a spiritual sense. Since we are in Christ, He sees what we have become. God accepts us based on this blended condition. It is like taking our sinful nature and placing it in the blender and pouring in Jesus. As a result, you have a new creation. Paul says, "To the praise of the glory of his grace, wherein he has made us accepted in the beloved" (Ephesians 1:6).

It took **the blood ransom** to cause all of this to happen. In Ephesians 1:7, Paul says, "In whom we have redemption through his blood, the forgiveness of sins, according to the riches of his grace." The word *redemption* (*apolutrosin*) carries the idea of deliverance or setting a man free by paying a ransom. In 1 Timothy 2:5-6, Paul said, "For there is one God, and one mediator between God and men, the man Christ Jesus; who gave himself a ransom for all, to be testified in due time."

Let me comment on **the bound released** as a result of the blood ransom. We were once in Satan's custody as we shall see in a moment. Jesus came and paid the ultimate price for our release. If that's not enough to excite you, although we are all guilty of sinning, the freedom comes with forgiveness of sins! The slate has been wiped clean and the record has been expunged! I am free and there are no more chains holding me. My soul is resting. It's just a blessing. Praise the Lord, hallelujah, I'm free. Yes, we were sentenced to death but the Judge came down from the bench and said, "I will die for him."

By the way, **the bridge reopened** between God and man when Jesus died for the sins of the world. Before Jesus died, there was not a way for humanity to return to God. We could not re-enter His presence because sin had erected a wall between us and God. The sin of the first Adam caused the bridge to close but the second Adam caused it to reopen.

Chapter 2

THE BLESSINGS CONTINUE
EPHESIANS 1:8-14

The Enlightened People
The Truth Received
The Transmitted Revelation
The Text Reviewed
The Thoughts Renewed
The Test Results
The Task Required
The Treasure Revealed

The Eschatological Process
The Coming Hour
The Controlled House
The Chaotic Habitation
The Collected Harvest

The Creator's Handiwork
The Christian's Heaven
The Continuous Hallelujahs

The Exit Plan
The Settled Score
The Secret Service
The Scenic Snapshots
The Saved Souls
The Shared Scripture
The Sealed Saints
The Stationed Spirit
The Surety Statement

EPHESIANS 1:3-14 IS probably the longest single sentence of unbroken discourse in ancient literature. It is really one long sentence dealing with the spiritual blessings for God's family. In the last chapter, I dealt with the first part of the sentence up to Ephesians 1:7. In that chapter, I covered some of the spiritual blessings we have as members of the family of God. We learned that we were chosen before the start of human existence. We were predestinated to be redeemed by Jesus serving as the ransom. We have been adopted and we have been forgiven. We have become blameless and holy due to the covering of Christ and our position in Him.

In this chapter, I want to focus on the second half of the sentence about the spiritual blessings for God's family. As noted before, we are not talking about material blessings that are temporal in this passage. We are dealing with spiritual blessings that are eternal.

THE ENLIGHTENED PEOPLE

As a result of **the truth received**, the people were enlightened. According to Ephesians 1:8, we have received wisdom from Him. The word *abounded* means more than enough! The word *wisdom* (*sophia*) means seeing and knowing truth. A wise person is able to grasp the great truths of life. James said, "If any of you lack wisdom, let him ask of God, that giveth to all men liberally, and upbraideth not; and it shall be given him" (James 1:5). This wisdom is only found in Jesus Christ and is promised only to those who search after Him. It deals with knowing the deep things of God

Therefore, wisdom is equivalent to **the transmitted revelation** from God. Godly wisdom involves passing or transmitting information. It is a divine revelation given to the redeemed people. It is what God desires for us to know. In 1 Corinthians 2:6-7, Paul said, "Howbeit we speak wisdom among them that are perfect: yet not the wisdom of this world, nor of the princes of this world, that come to nought: But we speak the wisdom of God in a mystery, even the hidden wisdom, which God ordained before the world unto our glory."

Let's deal with **the text reviewed** by believers. The wisdom from God is always tied to the Word of God. You have to continuously review the Word in order to be wise. We must study the Word of God frequently in order to be wise. Paul said, "Study to shew thyself approved unto God, a workman that needeth not to be ashamed, rightly dividing the word of truth" (2 Timothy 2:15). He later says, "And that from a child thou has known the holy scriptures, which are able to make thee *wise* unto salvation through faith which is in Christ Jesus" (2 Timothy 3:15, emphasis added).

A person cannot become enlightened without having **the thoughts renewed** based on the received Word. Once the truth is received, our mind becomes renewed. In Romans 12:2, Paul said, "And be not conformed to this world: but be ye transformed by the renewing of your mind, that ye may prove what is that good, and acceptable, and perfect, will of God." We can also see the difference when the Word was read before we were saved and we didn't get anything from it. It was just interesting reading. After enter the family, it takes on new meaning for us. It is due to the fact that your old thought process has been replaced with a new way of thinking.

It is difficult to deal with the issues of life without having wisdom from God. **The test results** will determine how wise the believer has become. A wise believer knows the answer when tempted or tested. When the test or temptation comes, the wise believer reflects on the Word studied. The wise believer remembers he has strength to do all things according to the Word of God. There is still a problem to address. As a wise believer, you can make a perfect score on the test but fail when it comes to acting on what you know. It is one thing to know the answer and another to apply it.

This is why Paul deals with **the task required** of the wise believer. He not only gives wisdom; he gives prudence (*phronesis*). Prudence means "seeing how to use and do the truth." In

Colossians 1:9, Paul said, "For this cause we also, since the day we heard it, do not cease to pray for you, and to desire that ye might be filled with the knowledge of his will in all wisdom and spiritual understanding." It is seeing the direction to take. It is having understanding, insight, and the ability to solve day-to-day problems. It is down-to-earth practical understanding. This deals with the practical response to the truth received. It is spiritual understanding. It is applying the nuts and bolts. Wisdom could be viewed as private information but understanding deals with practical application. This is the implementation of inspirational information. In 2 Timothy 2:7, Paul said, "Consider what I say; and the Lord give thee understanding in all things."

In Ephesians 1:9, Paul said, "Having made known unto us the mystery of his will, according to his good pleasure which he has purposed in himself." The mystery of His will deals with **the treasure revealed** to us. We have been spiritually blessed to have the mysteries of God revealed. In the Bible a mystery is not some mysterious or difficult thing to understand. It is a truth that has been locked up in God's plan for ages until He was ready to reveal it to man. When the time came, He unlocked the treasure or truth and opened it up to man. It was in His sovereign plan to one day open the treasure for us to see into the spiritual realm. In 1 Corinthians 2:10, Paul said, "But God hath revealed them unto us by his Spirit: for the Spirit searcheth all things, yea, the deep things of God."

THE ESCHATOLOGICAL PROCESS

Eschatology deals with the events related to the last days. Paul desires to remind us of **the coming hour** in this world. Paul speaks of the "dispensation of the fullness of times" in Ephesians 1:10. He is letting us in on the act that initiated the countdown of the coming climactic consummation. In a real sense, he is dealing with the hour that has come as well as the hour scheduled to come. Therefore, the dispensation of the fullness of time started when God sent His Son.

In Galatians 4:4-5, Paul said, "But when the fullness of the time was come, God sent forth his Son, made of a woman, made under his law, to redeem them that were under the law, that we might receive the adoption of sons." The hour of the Savior's arrival was planned long before the hour arrived. The same is true about the climactic conclusion of life as we know it. It is scheduled to happen.

Paul is also dealing with **the controlled house** in Ephesians 1:10. The word *dispensation* carries the meaning of "household arrangement" or "household management." The idea is that the universe is a house under the management of God. He really does have the whole world in His hands. He is not only the manager; He is the founder and owner. The psalmist said, "The earth is the Lord's, and the fullness thereof; the world, and they that dwell therein. For he hath founded it upon the seas, and established it upon the floods" (Psalm 24:1-2).

When you look at **the chaotic habitation**, you almost want to question God's management style. Let's continue to read what Paul says in Ephesians 1:10. He says, "In the dispensation of the fulness of times, God will gather together in one all things in Christ." If God is in control of the house, why is there so much chaos? For God to "gather together" means there is disharmony in the present existential realm. How could there be disharmony if God is the manager? God is a great house manager but He has some bad tenants. One day, He will clean house. He will "gather together in one all things in Christ." As chaotic as it is right now, it is hard for us to see how there will be harmony in the future. We must keep in mind that God will do it.

The other image projected by using the words *gather together* is connected to **the collected harvest**. There will be a day when the good crops will be separated from the bad crops. Every baptized and born-again believer will be gathered together with all other believers when the time comes. He will separate the wheat from the tares and the sheep from the goats. Jesus explains this in the parable of the wheat and tares. Both are growing up together right now, but a day of separation will come.

In Matthew 13:30, Jesus said, "Let both grow together until the harvest: and in the time of harvest I will say to the reapers, Gather ye together first the tares and bind them in bundles to burn them: but gather the wheat into my barn." In Matthew 13:49-50, Jesus said, "So shall it be at the end of the world: the angels shall come forth, and sever the wicked from among the just, and shall cast them into the furnace of fire: there shall be wailing and gnashing of teeth."

When I look at the Creator's handiwork, I cannot help but marvel over it. When I look at the stars in the sky and the moonlit night, it sends chills through my body as I think about God's power to create these things. You cannot help but look at the Creator's handiwork and find yourself in awe. However, in the words of my grandma, "We ain't seen nothing yet." When God starts gathering things together, it will blow our minds. In 1 Corinthians 2:9, Paul said, "But as it is written, Eye hath not seen, nor ear heard, neither have entered into the heart of man, the things which God hath prepared for them that love him."

Paul says, "In whom also we have obtained an inheritance, being predestinated according to the purpose of him who worketh all things after the counsel of his own will" (Ephesians 1:11). The inheritance of Ephesians 1:11 deals with the Christian's heaven that God prepared before anyone became a believer. John said, "I saw a new heaven and a new earth for the first heaven and the first earth were passed away; and there was no more sea" (Revelation 21:1).

Whenever I bring up the passage from the book of Revelation, someone will ask me: "Pastor, where are we going to be, in the new heaven or on the new earth?" My response is always the same. I explain the meaning of the word *heaven* in

Revelation 21:1. The new heaven is not dealing with the place where God resides. It is dealing with heavenly bodies (sun, moon, clouds, sky, planets, etc.). Although you will still have heaven and a new earth, I respond by saying, "We will be with God forever!" I don't care where we end up as long as we are with Him forever.

With this inheritance, we will be involved in an unending praise party. The day will come when **the continuous hallelujahs** flow from our mouths. Since we will be in His presence forever, Paul says, "that we should be to the praise of his glory, who first trusted in Christ" (Ephesians 1:12). As a result of trusting in Christ, we will one day witness the full glory of God who made it all possible. There will be nonstop praise taking place for what God has done. John was given an opportunity to see and hear future things connected to our eschatological hope. In Revelation 19:1, John said, "And after these things I heard a great voice of much people in heaven, saying, Alleluia; Salvation, and glory, and honour, and power, unto the Lord our God."

THE EXIT PLAN

In this passage, Paul is also informing us of **the settled score** that will take place with the enemy in the future. Satan knows that the day will come when God Almighty will put the house in order. He knows his days are numbered. This explains the increased assault from the enemy. He knows the clock is ticking and the end is nearer than ever before.

When will this transition from earth to glory take place for the church? When will we obtain the inheritance and spend eternity glorifying our God? When will God settle the score with Satan? No one can answer those questions because of **the secret service**. Earlier in the chapter, I shared how God opened the treasure chest and showed us the divine mysteries. Well, there is one treasure chest still locked up. When will the redemption of the purchased possession take place? We don't know when it will happen because this service will be kept in secret by God until it happens.

It is true that we do not know the hour but God has given us a sneak preview. Throughout the Bible, we are able to see **the scenic snapshots** of the eschatological process. He has spotlighted the scene to give us an idea of what will happen. It is like a trailer for a movie. It is not the entire movie, just enough to whet our appetites. What is interesting about this sneak preview is that it gives away the ending. In 1 Thessalonians 4:16-17, Paul says, "For the Lord himself shall descend from heaven with a shout, with the voice of the archangel, and with the trump of God: and the dead in Christ shall rise first: Then we which are alive and remain shall be caught up together with them in the clouds, to meet the Lord in the air: and so shall we ever be with the Lord." As chaotic as it is in this world, we are still seeing **the saved souls** added to the family of faith daily. It is true that the time will come for God to settle the score, but it will not happen until the predestinated souls are converted. In Ephesians 1:13, Paul says, "In whom ye also trusted. . . ." We should rejoice over the fact that we were included in the number.

We ended up trusting in Him because of **the shared Scripture** received on the journey. Paul says, "In whom ye also trusted, after that ye heard the word of truth, the gospel of your salvation" (Ephesians 1:13). We trusted in God after we heard the Word of Truth. We heard the "Word of Truth" after someone shared the Scripture with us. In reality, most of us heard the truth over and over again from different people in different places before we received the message. One day, the light came on and we accepted the truth shared.

As a result of receiving the gospel of our salvation, we immediately became **the sealed saints** of God. Yes, we have been sealed by the Holy Spirit. Paul said, "Who hath also sealed us, and given the earnest of the Spirit in our hearts" (2 Corinthians 1:22).

The next point is obvious but worth mentioning. Since we have been sealed until the day of redemption, we have **the stationed Spirit** with us. When the Spirit of God comes into the believer's life, He is there to stay. You cannot lose the Holy Spirit if you have received Him. He is stationed in the life of all believers. No action of the believer can cause Him to depart. We can cause Him to be grieved but He does not exit the life of a believer.

Look at **the surety statement** in Ephesians 1:14. Paul says, "Which is the earnest of our inheritance until the redemption of the purchased possession, unto the praise of his glory." The presence and power of the Holy Spirit is the "earnest of our inheritance." It is like the earnest money paid to show your sincerity regarding the purchase of property. In the past, the earnest money given meant that it was a done deal but there were a few steps to work out before the transaction was completed. It was a guarantee of performance. The rest is coming later. Therefore, the earnest of inheritance is connected to work of the Spirit assuring us of the done deal.

The Holy Spirit let us know that the deal is done. In Romans 8:16, Paul said, "The Spirit itself beareth witness with our spirit, that we are the children of God." In Galatians 4:6, he says, "And because ye are sons, God hath sent forth the Spirit of his Son into your hearts, crying, Abba, Father."

DO YOU KNOW HIM?

EPHESIANS 1:15-23

DO YOU KNOW Him? A lot of people know about Him but they don't really know Him. I am speaking of an experiential knowledge and not an intellectual knowledge. It involves knowing Him in an intimate way.

He said, "I heard . . ." Paul starts off Ephesians 1:15 dealing with **the circulated talk** about the family of faith in Ephesus. Let's not forget where Paul is writing this letter from. He is under house arrest in Rome and he says, "I have heard some things about you." A lot of what Paul heard was based on his inquiry. When saints visited him in prison, he had to inquire about the churches God used him to plant. He wanted to see them again but circumstances prevented it from happening. He had to be excited about what he heard concerning the believers there. What is the talk circulating about you? What have people heard about you?

He had heard about **the Christian testimony** of the saints in Ephesus. He said, "After I heard of your faith in the Lord Jesus . . ." (Ephesians 1:15).

Your testimony should be so strong that it is buzzed throughout the region where you reside. People in your neighborhood should know that Christians live at that address. People should know that a Christian sits at that desk in the workplace. We are justified by faith. Paul said, "Therefore being justified by faith, we have peace with God through our Lord Jesus Christ" (Romans 5:1). Before Paul's life comes to an end, he will say, "I have fought a good fight, I have finished my course, I have kept the faith" (2 Timothy 4:7). We usually read these remarks as three separate acts of Paul. However, the Greek text paints a different picture. "I was able to fight a good fight and finish my course because I kept the faith."

The common thread for Christians is revealed in this verse. Christians have put their faith in the Lord Jesus (not Buddha, Muhammad, Confucius, etc.). There is no other name that can lead to salvation. It is our "faith in the Lord Jesus" that creates the family of faith. It was through faith by grace that we became a part of the family. It had nothing to do with works as we shall see later in this study. This is the tie that binds our hearts together in Christian love. In the next chapter, Paul will say, "For by grace are ye saved through faith; and that not of yourselves: it is the gift of God" (Ephesians 2:8). It is a gift we did not deserve. We deserved to die in our sins but God chose to give us the gift of salvation. Paul said, "For the wages of sin is death; but the gift of God is eternal life through Jesus Christ our Lord" (Romans 6:23).

The caring test is a great way to authenticate the connection to the family of God. Paul had also heard that they were ministering to the saints of God. They had love for the saints. How can you love a God you have never seen and hate the people you see daily? John said, "If a man say, I love God, and hateth his brother, he is a liar: for he that loveth not his brother whom he hath seen, how can he love God whom he hath not seen? And this commandment have we from him, That he who loveth God loveth his brother also" (1 John 4:20-21).

The saints in Ephesus were demonstrating great love for God's people, which is one of the greatest signs of our connection to Him. Jesus said, "A new commandment I give unto you, that ye love one another; as I have loved you, that ye also love one another. By this shall all men know that ye are my disciples, if ye have love one to another" (John 13:34-35).

Yes, we are to demonstrate our connection to God by loving one another. Yet **the challenging task** of loving people comes up in this verse. The faith in Jesus creates the tie but it is the second part of Ephesians 1:15 that I find to be the most challenging. He heard of their love unto *all* of the saints. The love was for all of the saints (even the ones who were not easy to love). This love is called "*agape.*" You can even love your enemies when agape is attached to your life. It is unconditional. It is the 1 Corinthians 13 kind of love (see 1 Corinthians 13:4-5). This kind of love suffers long and is kind.

Paul says, "[I] cease not to give thanks for you, making mention of you in my prayers" (Ephesians 1:16). When Paul mentions **the ceaseless thanks,** he is not merely thanking God for their salvation. For this he was thankful, but his gratitude dealt with much more. Why would he always thank God for them? He thanked God that there were other people committed and involved in kingdom building. Their commitment to Christ and His church caused him to be thankful for them while he was in prison. He was thankful for the work that continued in his absence.

It is important to tie the ceaseless thanks with **the contacted throne**. When Paul prayed, he talked to God about the believers at Ephesus. Paul prayed all the time. In 1 Thessalonians, Paul said, "Pray without ceasing" (1 Thessalonians 5:17). He was informing them that he continued to be in contact with the throne of God on their behalf. We are to pray without ceasing for the church. Every time we pray, we should include the church (local and global) in our prayers.

Now let's examine **the chosen topic** of his petition. He was praying that "the God of our Lord Jesus Christ, the Father of glory, may give unto you the spirit of wisdom and revelation in the knowledge of him" (Ephesians 1:17). He wasn't praying for them to be exempt from trials or tribulation. Neither did he pray for them to prosper financially. He prayed for them to grow in the knowledge of God.

In essence, Paul prayed that the believers in Ephesus would become more knowledgeable of the Father by getting to know the Scriptures and the Savior. The God we are to know is the God of Jesus Christ, the Father of glory. We are to know the God Jesus worshipped while on earth. We are to know the God Jesus showed us while here on earth. In John 14:8-9, Philip said to him, "Lord, show us the Father, and it sufficeth us. Jesus saith unto him, Have I been so long with you, and yet hast thou not known me, Philip? He that hath seen me hath seen the Father; and how sayest thou then, show us the Father?"

In Ephesians 1:17, we have one of those rare verses mentioning **the combined Trinity**. Knowledge of God must come from God. There is no other God. We are to know the Father of glory, the only true and living God (the Supreme Majesty and Sovereign Lord of the universe). Paul described Him as "the God of our Lord Jesus Christ, the Father of glory" (Ephesians 1:17). In 1 Corinthians 2:7-8, Jesus is described as the "Lord of glory." Paul said, "But we speak the wisdom of God in a mystery, even the hidden wisdom, which God ordained before the world unto our glory: Which none of the princes of this world knew: for had they known it, they would not have crucified *the Lord of glory*" (emphasis added). In 1 Corinthians 2:10, Paul says, "But God hath revealed them unto us by his Spirit" (1 Corinthians 2:10a). Therefore, God, the Holy Spirit, is the revealer of glory.

After salvation, **the convert's training** is vitally important. Paul prayed that "the God of our Lord Jesus Christ, the Father of glory, may give unto you the spirit of wisdom and revelation in the knowledge of him" (Ephesians 1:17). It is true that faith in our Lord Jesus leads to conversion. Once conversion comes into our lives, we need to learn as much as possible about the one who converted us. The spirit of wisdom and revelation causes the believer to have a working knowledge that leads to growth.

The comprehended truth is the key to spiritual growth. One day, I stood before the Sunday school class as a teenager and recited John 14 in its entirety. The students and teacher started clapping. After class, when the other students departed, my teacher said, "I know you know what the chapter says. Do you know what it means?" I could not answer her question. We have received the Truth (Jesus Christ) when we were converted and now we need to know the truth in order to operate in the freedom that comes with it. Jesus said, "Ye shall know the truth, and the truth shall make you free" (John 8:32). It is like the story about the Ethiopian eunuch in Acts 8. He was reading the Scripture and could probably recite the passage verbatim that he read from Isaiah. Yet he did not comprehend it. God sent a deacon by the name of Philip to explain the meaning of the passage. When the Ethiopian eunuch comprehended the truth, he responded accordingly (see Acts 8:32-39).

I am amazed by **the continuous thirst** that comes when a believer desires to know God in an intimate way. He desires to give the spirit of wisdom and revelation "in the knowledge of him"

(Ephesians 1:17b). You can't get enough of this knowledge. The more you learn, the more you desire to know. The psalmist said, "I stretch forth my hands unto thee: my soul thirsteth after thee, as a thirsty land" (Psalm 143:6). Jesus said, "Blessed are they which do hunger and thirst after righteousness: for they shall be filled" (Matthew 5:6).

The proof of the growing knowledge is seen in **the creature's transformation**. As we learn truth from God's Word and apply it to our lives, our character and conduct change. It is the comprehension of truth that transforms us into the new creations that Paul talked about in 2 Corinthians 5:17. Paul says, "Therefore if any man be in Christ, he is a new creature: old things are passed away; behold, all things are become new." We begin to see the spiritual transformation occurring as the comprehended Word takes over in our lives.

Wise and knowledgeable Christians have **the created torch** for their journey. The knowledge of the Word creates a light to shine in the darkness. As a result of the spirit of wisdom and revelation in the knowledge of Him, Paul says, "The eyes of your understanding being enlightened; that ye may know what is the hope of his calling, and what the riches of the glory of his inheritance in the saints" (Ephesians 1:18).

The psalmist said, "For thou wilt light my candle: the Lord my God will enlighten my darkness" (Psalm 18:28). Paul said, "For God, who commanded the light to shine out of darkness, hath shined in our hearts to give light of the knowledge of the glory of God in the face of Jesus Christ" (2 Corinthians 4:6). The psalmist said, "The entrance of thy words giveth light; it giveth understanding unto the simple" (Psalm 119:130). This is when His Word becomes a lamp unto our feet and a light unto our pathway. I don't have to be the smartest person in the world to carry this torch.

We need this torch to deal with **the coming temptations** from the enemy. We will deal with some of the temptations later on in this study, but Paul wanted them to have the spiritual insight to face the coming temptations. As a result of the wisdom, knowledge, and enlightened hearts, saints become aware of the devices and schemes set up by the enemy.

We will learn how to deal with the tricks, traps, and temptations when we study the last chapter of Ephesians. In this passage, Paul deals with **the concentrated thoughts** of the believer. We must stay focused on the hope of His calling and the riches of the glory of His inheritance in the saints (see Ephesians 1:18c). Let me explain the word *hope* in the text. It is not used the same way we normally use the term. When we say, "I hope it will happen," we are dealing with the possibility of something happening. It may or may not take place. However, the word in the text deals with "assured expectancy."

God has called us to stand before Him in the name and righteousness of Jesus Christ as His righteous, blameless, and holy inheritance. When that glorious day of redemption comes, we shall be made just like our Lord Jesus Christ. We are His inheritance. In Ephesians 1:19, Paul said, "And what is the exceeding greatness of his power to us-ward who believe, according to the working of his mighty power" (Ephesians 1:19). While concentrating on Him and waiting for Him to come, we have the greatness of His power to help us. The exceeding greatness of His power means it is (*megathos*) mighty and explosive.

The Christian's transcendence is based solely on "the working of his mighty power" (Ephesians 1:19). As a result of witnessing His power, you are capable of transcending. The word *transcend* means you can go beyond the limits due to the greatness of His power. I can now do all things through Christ who strengthens me. This ability to go beyond the limits is seen with the clever traps mentioned earlier. Paul said, "There hath no temptation taken you but such as is common to man: but God is faithful, who will not suffer you to be tempted above that ye are able; but will with the temptation also make a way to escape, that ye may be able to bear it" (1 Corinthians 10:13).

You are able to transcend by the power of Christ rather than your own strength. Paul said, "And he said unto me, my grace is sufficient for thee: for my strength is made perfect in weakness. Most gladly therefore will I rather glory in my infirmities, that the power of Christ may rest upon me" (2 Corinthians 12:9).

The Calvary trip should be taken in order to see how this all happened. Paul explains how great this power is by taking us back to the first Easter weekend. In speaking of this power in Ephesians 1:20a, Paul said, "Which he wrought in Christ, when he raised him from the dead. . . ." Paul is saying if you want to see this power in action, go to Calvary for a moment. They had beaten Christ until His face was barely recognizable. They had scourged Him until the lacerations on His back revealed His bones. They had crowned Him with thorns so that blood poured down His head like a flowing stream. They nailed Him to a wooden cross by driving spikes in His hands and feet and they hung Him up to die.

Agonizing moments crept on until, after six hours of this torment, He dismissed His Spirit, bowed His head, and died. The Roman soldier made sure He was dead by taking a spear and stabbing Him. There was additional proof of His death by Nicodemus and the women who bathed His mortal remains in spices and bandages. His dead body was locked up in a borrowed tomb, but early that Sunday morning, God raised Him with all power in His hands.

Following the trip to Calvary, the crowning time arrived. The same power that raised Him from the dead also elevated Him to the top position of authority. He has the highest seat of honor and authority in the universe (both the spiritual and physical realms). In Ephesians 1:20b-22a, Paul said, "And set him at his own right hand in the heavenly places. Far above all principality and power, and might, and dominion, and every name that is named, not only in this world, but also in that which is to come; and has put all things under his feet. . . ."

In an act of mockery, they placed a sign over Jesus' head that said, "This is Jesus the King of the Jews." The sign should have said, "King of kings." Peter said, "Who is gone into heaven, and is on the right hand of God; angels and authorities and powers being made subject unto him" (1 Peter 3:22). Check out what He is doing in this position of authority at this time. In Acts 5:30-31, Peter said, "The God of our fathers raised up Jesus, whom ye slew and hanged on a tree. Him hath God exalted with his right hand to be Prince and a Saviour, for to give repentance to Israel, and forgiveness of sins." He is saving people in His exalted position.

He reminds us of **the clock ticking.** If He has the highest seat of honor and authority, why hasn't He addressed this corruption? Don't forget that the clock is still ticking. Paul said, "Wherefore God also hath highly exalted him, and given him a name which is above every name: That at the name of Jesus every knee should bow, of things in heaven, and things in earth, and things under the earth" (Philippians 2:9-10).

Paul concludes this chapter by telling us, "[God] gave him to be head over all things to the church, Which is his body, the fulness of him that filleth all in all" (Ephesians 1:22b-23). These verses deal with **the Commander's team,** the church. Christ paid the supreme price to start and build the church: He died for it. As a result, God has given Him the supreme position over the church. We are not talking about the building but the body.

The church is called the "body of Christ." It is the picture of the human body with Christ being the head. A head must have a body to carry out the plans transmitted from the head. In Romans 12:5, Paul said, "So we, being many, are one body in Christ, and every one members one of another." The church completes all for Christ. Jesus Christ is working throughout the world and in human history to bring about God's eternal plan for the world. He is working and fitting everything into its proper place, and He is doing it through the church.

Chapter 4

THE BEFORE AND AFTER LOOK

EPHESIANS 2:1-7

The Past Pattern	The Present Position
The Background Story	The Available Mercy
The Bequeathed Separation	The Agape Move
The Born Sinner	The Amazing Miracle
The Blameworthy Source	The Advocate's Mission
The Bondage System	The Added Message
The Backward Steps	The Acknowledged Mediator
The Blended Spirits	The Accepted Messiah
The Blinded State	The Altered Mind
The Behavioral System	The Assembled Multitude
The Bad Side	
The Banning Sentence	

THE BOOK OF Ephesians paints a picture of God's redemptive purpose. Paul shows how man's spiritual problems were settled once and for all by Jesus Christ. Only God could fix the great divide that existed between Himself and the crown of His creation, mankind. In this section of Ephesians, Paul shows us the way we looked before Christ came into our hearts. He also shows us what happened in our lives after God allowed His Son to serve as the ultimate sacrifice.

THE PAST PATTERN

Paul says, "And you hath he quickened, who were dead in trespasses and sins" (Ephesians 2:1). Before we were quickened (brought to life), we had issues. We should never forget the background story that existed before salvation. All of us came to God with the same issue connected to the past. It was the sin issue. We were all sinners in need of the Savior in our lives. Even though I may not know you, our past story is pretty much the same from a spiritual perspective. We were born sinners.

He succinctly says, "We were dead!" This deals with the bequeathed separation. Since Adam sinned, death has been passed down. "For since by man came death, by man came also the resurrection of the dead. For as in Adam all die, even so in Christ shall all be made alive" (1 Corinthians 15:21-22). How can a man be living and yet be dead? The basic meaning of death (*nekros*) is *separation*. Therefore, death means that a person is separated, either separated from his body or from God or from both.

- **The Physical Death:** the separation of a man's spirit from his body. It is when a person ceases to exist on earth and is buried. "And as it is appointed unto men once to die, but after this the judgment" (Hebrews 9:27).

- **The Spiritual Death:** the separation of a man from God while he is still living and walking upon earth. This is the natural state of a man on earth without Christ. Man is seen as still in his sins and dead to God. "But she that liveth in pleasure is dead while she liveth" (1 Timothy 5:6). Do you remember what the father said to the other son when the prodigal son came home? He said, "It was meet that we should make merry, and be glad: for this thy brother was dead, and is alive again; and was lost, and is found" (Luke 15:32).

- **The Eternal Death (Second Death):** It is the eternal state of being dead or separated from God. When Paul was speaking about the Lord's return and those who do not know God, he said, "Who shall be punished with everlasting destruction from the presence of the Lord, and from the glory of his power" (2 Thessalonians 1:9).

I always like to make this point clear. We were dead in trespasses and sins. Let's look at **the born sinners** for a moment. The Greek word translated "trespasses" is *paratoma*, which means "a falling aside when one was designed to stand upright." It conveys the idea of falling aside from truth and uprightness. We were also dead in sins. The word translated "sins" is derived from *hamartono*, which means "to miss the mark, to wander from the right path, to go the wrong way, to do the wrong thing." We did not become sinners after committing our first sin. We were born sinners and the act of sin was due to the birth status. This is what David was speaking of when he said, "Behold, I was shapen in iniquity; and in sin did my mother conceive me" (Psalm 51:5).

Paul says, "Wherein in time past ye walked according to the course of this world, according to the prince of the power of the air, the spirit that now worketh in the children of disobedience" (Ephesians 2:2). We walked according to the "prince of the power of the air." Paul reveals **the blameworthy source** of our past condition. I often say, "The devil can't make us do anything without our consent." This statement is for the believer. However, in times past, it was not the case. The prince of the power of the air controlled us and we did not have a power source with which to combat him.

The reason we walked according to the "prince of the power of the air" was due to **the bondage system** that existed. We received our marching orders from the one ruling our lives. Paul actually uses the phrase "prince of the power of the air" to teach against the doctrine of an anti-Christian heresy called Gnosticism. The Gnostic heretic believed the universe was ruled by many intermediaries or emanations (*aeons*) of deity that stood between God and man. As a result of intellect and learning, they believed people could achieve acceptance with God. Therefore, Paul is saying that there are powers in the air but not as the Gnostics described. The prince (*archon*) of the power (*exousia*) of the air ruled the air. We were in bondage. Satan ruled our lives. John said, "He that commits sin is of the devil: for the devil sinned from the beginning . . . " (1 John 3:8a).

Since we were born in sin, we came into this world walking in the wrong direction. Once again, **the backward steps** resulted from the leader in our lives. Which way did we go? We walked according to the course of this world. Instead of walking toward God, we were walking backward. Before Christ, we walked backwards on a one-way street that led straight to hell. It is true that heaven existed, but the road had not been constructed for humanity to head in that direction. All humanity traveled on the road that led to death and destruction.

Before Christ, **the blended spirits** of humanity and Satan caused us to live in sin. Sin was natural because it was a part of our nature. As a result of Satan being in charge and in control, our spirits were infected by him. There was a spirit of disobedience that caused us to do what we did. Disobedience was in our spiritual DNA and we didn't have the power to do anything about it.

The blind state of existence prevented us from seeing God. We were blinded by the prince of the power of the air. Paul said, "But if our gospel be hid, it is hid from them that are lost: in whom the god of this world hath blinded the minds of them which believe not, lest the light of the glorious gospel of Christ, who is the image of God, should shine unto them" (2 Corinthians 4:3-4). Yes, we were walking in total darkness and the light of God's glory was hidden from us.

The behavioral system is linked to the belief system. You behave based on what you believe. If you don't believe in God, you will not behave godly. No one ever has to teach a child to misbehave. It comes naturally. This is why we have to teach obedience and reinforce the teaching repeatedly. Paul said, "The spirit that now worketh in the children of disobedience: Among whom also we all had our conversation in times past . . ." (Ephesians 2:2b-3a). The Greek word rendered "children" means "son" and has specific reference to one's origin, nature, and relationship to his father. We were heirs of this disobedient spirit. Jesus said, "Ye are of your father the devil and the lusts of your father, ye will do. He was a murderer from the beginning, and abode not in the truth, because there is no truth in him. When he speaketh a lie, he speaketh of his own: for he is a liar, and the father of it" (John 8:44).

Paul said, "Among whom also we all had our conversation in times past in the lusts of our flesh, fulfilling the desires of the flesh and of the mind" (Ephesians 2:3). The flesh is considered **the bad side** of our design. Every person has this side. This is what Paul meant by "lusts of our flesh." The Greek word translated "lusts" is *epithumia,* meaning "strong desire," not necessarily evil. You can strongly desire good or bad things. In this case, Paul is referencing the bad connected to the depravity of humanity. Since the flesh and mind were controlled by the prince of the power of the air (the prince of this world), our strong desires were not toward God. It is a natural desire for the things of this world only.

In the past, we were controlled by natural desire. Paul told us in Romans 3:20 that no flesh shall be justified in His sight.

In Romans 7:18, Paul said, "For I know that in me (that is, in my flesh,) dwells *no* good thing (emphasis added)." In Romans 8:5, he said, "For they that are after the flesh do mind the things of the flesh." In Romans 8:13, he also said, "If we live after the flesh, we shall die." John said, "For all that is in the world, the lust of the flesh, and the lust of the eyes, and the pride of life, is not of the Father, but is of the world" (1 John 2:16).

Due to Satan's control of humanity, **the banning sentence** was rendered by God. "We were by nature the children of wrath, even as others" (Ephesians 2:3). We were all sentenced and destined to receive the wrath and justice of God. We all deserved the wrath of God. We were dead, damned, and doomed. We were scheduled to be banned from the presence of God forever.

When God looked at humanity, He could only see dark souls covered with sins and trespasses. This made it impossible to dwell or reside in the presence of God. Paul said, "For the wrath of God is revealed from heaven against all ungodliness and unrighteousness of men, who hold the truth in unrighteousness" (Romans 1:18).

Let's go back to 2 Thessalonians again. Paul said, "And to you who are troubled rest with us, when the Lord Jesus shall be revealed from heaven with his mighty angels, in flaming fire taking vengeance on them that know not God, and that obey not the gospel of our Lord Jesus Christ" (2 Thessalonians 1:7-8).

THE PRESENT POSITION

I am glad Paul didn't stop writing at Ephesians 2:3. If he had stopped writing, we wouldn't know about **the available mercy** revealed in Ephesians 2:4. Paul said, "But God who is rich in mercy. . . ." We were destined to receive the wrath of God, but God. . . . A lot of sermons have been delivered about this conjunction in the passage. Thank God for the conjunction "but."

God is rich in mercy. Mercy means: feelings of pity, compassion, affection, and kindness. The psalmist said, "Thou has taken away all thy wrath: thou hast turned thyself from the fierceness of thine anger. . . . Shew us thy mercy, O Lord, and grant us thy salvation" (Psalm 85:3, 7). In the next section of the same psalm, the psalmist said, "But thou, O Lord, art a God full of compassion, and gracious, long suffering, and plenteous in mercy and truth" (Psalm 86:15).

The agape move of God led to our deliverance. It was his "great love" that caused the mercy to be applied. God is full of mercy and full of love. He is full of *agape*: a selfless and sacrificial love. It is a love that loves a person even if he doesn't deserve to be loved. We were unworthy but His great love saved us. John said, "For God so loved the world, that he gave his only begotten Son, that whosoever believeth in him should not perish, but have everlasting life" (John 3:16). "But God commendeth his love toward us, in that, while we were yet sinners, Christ died for us" (Romans 5:8).

Paul says, "Even when we were dead in sins, hath quickened us together with Christ, (by grace ye are saved)" (Ephesians 2:5). His mercy and love led to **the amazing miracle** of salvation. Although we were dead, God has quickened us together with Christ. The word *quickened* means to be made alive. This is a case of divine resuscitation. Not only were we divinely resuscitated, we have witnessed a full recovery after being dead so long. Paul is painting a picture of Jesus' death, burial, and resurrection. Just like Jesus died, we were dead. Just as God raised Jesus from the dead, He has done the same for those of us who believe.

This amazing miracle points to **the Advocate's mission**. Jesus Christ was the divine Advocate on a special mission for the Father. We know He came to die for sinners but He also came to deal with Satan. Let's go back to 1 John. John said, "He that commits sin is of the devil: for the devil sinned from the beginning. For this purpose the Son of God was manifested, that he might destroy the works of the devil "(1 John 3:8).

Look at **the added message** at the end of Ephesians 2:5. We are saved by grace. The applied mercy and love kept us from witnessing the wrath of God. The added message is that grace saved us. The parenthetical point in the verse is important. Yes, we were saved by His amazing grace! In Romans, Paul says, "For all have sinned, and come short of the glory of God; being justified freely by his grace [not good works] through the redemption that is in Christ Jesus" (Romans 3:23-24). It is merely an act of faith on our end. Jesus Christ did it all for us to be resuscitated. When a person truly believes in Jesus Christ, God loves His Son so much that He counts the person's belief as his identification with Christ. Paul said, "To wit, that God was in Christ, reconciling the world unto himself, not imputing their trespasses unto them; and hath committed unto us the word of reconciliation" (2 Corinthians 5:19).

There are a few points that I want to mention here but fully develop later on in this study. The first point to highlight here is connected to **the acknowledged Mediator** by the recipients of salvation. Jesus must be acknowledged as the Mediator who came to bridge the gap between man and God. He's the bridge to get us back to the Father. No one can be saved from his sins without acknowledging Jesus Christ as the Son of God who came to die for the sins of the world.

The next point to highlight is connected to **the accepted Messiah.** The ones who have been quickened together are the ones who have accepted the Messiah. The doctrine of universal salvation is not biblical. This doctrine infers that all people are saved as a result of the death, burial, and resurrection of Jesus Christ. This doctrine implies that man is not required to do anything to receive the gift of salvation because he is automatically covered. In Romans 10:9-10, Paul says, "That if thou shalt confess with thy mouth the Lord Jesus, and shalt believe in thine heart that

God hath raised him from the dead, thou shalt be saved. For with the heart man believeth unto righteousness; and with the mouth confession is made unto salvation."

The last point to highlight in this chapter is connected to **the altered mind** that follows the acceptance of Christ. The mind of the one who truly believes in Jesus Christ becomes altered as we shall see later. In 1 Corinthians 2:16, Paul says, "We have the mind of Christ." The mind is no longer controlled by Satan (the prince of the power of the air). Before knowing Christ, the mind of man is focused on this world only. The mind is focused on living large on this side and doing whatever it takes for it to happen. The mind of the unbeliever focuses on gaining the "whole world" with no concern about the soul. The opposite is true for the believer. The believer loves God with all his soul, mind, and strength (see Matthew 22:37 and Mark 12:30). The mind of the believer focuses on the Spirit rather than the flesh (see Romans 8:4-6).

Let's close this chapter dealing with **the assembled multitude**. Check out where the multitude comprising the church is presently assembled. According to Ephesians 2:6, He "hath raised us up together, and made us sit together in heavenly places in Christ Jesus." The believer is said to be "in Christ." Christ is said to be "in heaven sitting at the right hand of the Father." Therefore, all true believers are presently seated in heaven in Christ. As believers, we physically live on earth, but spiritually we have already been placed "in the heavenlies." I actually have two realms or addresses: one in Dallas County and the other in heaven in Christ. The one in Dallas County is temporary. As a matter of fact, from a spiritual perspective, I am not a citizen of Dallas County. Peter said, "Dearly beloved, I beseech you as strangers and pilgrims, abstain from fleshly lusts" (1 Peter 2:11). Since we are pilgrims and strangers, we don't need to get caught up in what the world has to offer.

SAVED AND SANCTIFIED TO SERVE
EPHESIANS 2:8-10

The Unmerited Reward
The Father's Response
The Favor Received
The Flawed Rebels
The Fall Reversed
The Felon's Record
The Fellowship Restored
The Faith Required
The Futile Route
The Fact Recorded

The Unearned Redemption
The Bridge Prepared
The Best Performance
The Birthmark Present

The Beguiling Prince
The Belittling Process
The Boasting Prohibited
The Buried Power

The Unbelievable Results
The Providential Workmanship
The Positional Worth
The Practiced Ways
The Participant's Walk
The Provided Word
The People Watching
The Progressive Work
The Preferred Worlds

ARE YOU SAVED and sanctified? I am not really asking you if you attend church regularly or work with some ministry. Have you accepted the free gift of salvation from God? This is the only way to be saved. If you are saved and sanctified, God didn't save and sanctify you just so you could one day enter the pearly gates. Yes, you will spend eternity with Him if you are saved and sanctified. However, you have been saved and sanctified to serve in this season on this side. Serving cannot save you but once you are saved, you will serve.

THE UNMERITED REWARD

Salvation resulted from **the Father's response** to our sinful condition. In Ephesians 2:8, Paul says, "For by grace are ye saved through faith; and that not of yourselves: it is the gift of God." Salvation is the work of God. We are saved today because the Father responded to our sin-sickness with His great love and rich mercy toward us. It is all about what the Father was willing to do for us.

Salvation is all about **the favor received**. Paul said, "For by grace are ye saved." As mentioned before, grace deals with the favor and kindness of God. This is why His grace is so amazing. The road to redemption was constructed by God and not man. God paved the way for man to come back to Him. We are believers today simply due to being gripped by God's grace.

The favor was received by **the flawed rebels**. The favor is unique in that it is not contingent on any good action of the recipient. It is not a favor based on another favor. You did me a favor so I will return the favor. Also, we grant favors based on whether or not it is deserved. Everyone receiving His grace or favor did so as a flawed recipient and rebel. His grace, favor, and kindness are given despite the fact that they are undeserved and unmerited. God has given us His grace despite our rejection of Him and rebellion against Him.

As a result of receiving His favor, we are saved (for by grace are ye saved). In this context, salvation actually deals with reversing the previous action. We have **the fall reversed** by one man's act of obedience. This is what Paul meant when he said, "For as by one man's disobedience many were made sinners, so by the obedience of one shall many be made righteous" (Romans 5:19). It is like taking a fall and God pushed "rewind" so that you are no longer down.

Not only has the fall of man been reversed, **the felon's record** has changed. Not only has God set us free from the bondage of sin, He has expunged our record. God said, "I, even I, am he that blotteth out thy transgressions for mine own sake, and will not remember thy sins" (Isaiah 43:25). The writer of Hebrews said, "And their sins and iniquities will I remember no more" (Hebrews 10:17).

Grace led to having **the fellowship restored** between man and God. Not only does it deal with reversing an action, it deals with restoring one back to the original design. We were dead in trespasses and sin but God rescued and restored us. Sin caused the image of God in our lives to be taken away. Salvation restored that image (*imago dei*). Peter said, "Whereby are given unto us exceeding great and precious promises: that by these ye might be partakers of the divine nature, having escaped the corruption that is in the world through lust" (2 Peter 1:4).

Let's look at **the faith required** for a person to be saved. You cannot be saved without believing what God did for you to be saved. Faith is mandatory. Without faith, it is impossible to please God. Let's take a trip to Calvary to see one of the greatest examples of this act of faith. It was a move of faith at Calvary that caused one of the dying thieves to make it in. He acknowledged Jesus as the King of kings when he said, "Lord, remember me when thou comest into thy kingdom" (Luke 23:42). This move of faith caused Jesus to say, "Verily I say unto thee, Today shalt thou be with me in paradise" (Luke 23:43).

We are saved by grace through faith; "and that not of yourselves" (Ephesians 2:8). Let's not forget that Paul is also speaking against **the futile route** of the Gnostic during the time of this writing. The Gnostic believed the way to God was through intellect and self-effort. The heresy basically taught that if a person knew enough and worked on personal improvement, he could achieve acceptance with God. Paul makes it perfectly clear that we did not and could not do anything to save ourselves. You did not and could not lift yourself from the fallen state.

The fact recorded at the end of Ephesians 2:8 clears up the matter. Salvation is God's gift. Paul tells us that it is the gift of God. It is a gift that none of us deserved. In Romans, Paul made it clear when he said, "For the wages of sin is death; but the gift of God is eternal life through Jesus Christ our Lord" (Romans 6:23). The wages of sin is death (what we all deserved) but God decided to give us the gift of salvation. Paul said, "Therefore as by the offence of one judgment came upon all men to condemnation; even so by the righteousness of one the free gift came upon all men unto justification of life" (Romans 5:18).

THE UNEARNED REDEMPTION

Paul says, "Not of works, lest any man should boast. For we are his workmanship created in Christ Jesus unto good works, which God hath before ordained that we should walk in them" (Ephesians 2:9-10). Jesus serves as **the bridge prepared** for us to cross over to God. There is no other way. Other religions teach that you can be saved by doing different things. The gift causes us to become saved and sanctified but we must not become so sanctimonious that we forget who caused it to happen.

The best performance of man could not measure up to God's standard. It is a gift from God that is not based on your performance (not of works). Your best performance could not lead to salvation. According to Isaiah 64:6, "All our righteousness is as filthy rags." Paul said, "Not by works of righteousness which we have done, but according to his mercy he saved us, by the washing of regeneration, and renewing of the Holy Ghost" (Titus 3:5).

The birthmark present in all of our lives (sin) automatically voided any possibility for us to do anything to be saved. Even if we could perform all good works (which we can't), the birthmark of sin would have prevented us from being saved. We were born as sinners. We have already discussed how we were all born dead in trespasses and sins. Good works cannot change the spiritual birth defect. This would be like washing dirty clothes in dirty water. The clothes would still end up dirty. Don't forget that sin is not simply connected to what you do. It involves what you say and think. For instance, you may never engage in the acts of fornication or adultery but if you have lust in your heart and mind, you have sinned. Sin was in all of us from the start.

Don't forget about **the beguiling prince** who controlled us before Christ. There is a power greater than you named in the passage as the prince of the power of the air. He has already deceived you if you think you can earn salvation by working for it. He continues to trick and deceive you. In Romans 10, Paul addressed this self-righteous approach. He said, "Brethren, my heart's desire and prayer to God for Israel is, that they might be saved. For I bear them record that they have a zeal of God, but not according to knowledge. For they being ignorant of God's righteousness, and going about to establish their own righteousness, have not submitted themselves unto the righteousness of God" (Romans 10:1-3).

The self-righteous approach leads to **the belittling process**. When you think you can work enough to be saved, you reach a point in which others are belittled by you. It is like the Pharisee and the publican in the temple praying in Luke 18. Check out the Pharisee in Luke 18:11-12. Jesus said, "The Pharisee stood and prayed thus with himself, God, I thank thee, that I am not as other men are, extortioners, unjust, adulterers, or even as this publican. I fast twice in the week, I give tithes of all that I possess" (Luke 18:11-12). Now check out the publican. Jesus said, "And the publican, standing afar off, would not lift up so much as his eyes unto heaven, but smote upon his breast, saying, God be merciful to me a citizen" (Luke 18:13). Guess which one left the temple justified?

Since we didn't save ourselves, Paul says, "Not of works, lest any man should boast" (Ephesians 2:9). **The boasting prohibited** makes sense to me. No one has the right to boast because we didn't save ourselves. Jesus said, "He that speaketh of himself seeketh his own glory: but he that seeketh his glory that sent him, the same is true, and no unrighteousness is in him" (John 7:18). This is why Christians shouldn't walk around in pride or deceit in a spirit of arrogance.

We should behave like **the buried power** within us. We are sanctified and set apart by having the Spirit settled in us. We have a power buried within us that causes us not to boast. As a matter of fact, the Holy Spirit will not boast of Himself. Jesus said, "But when the Comforter is come, whom I will send unto you from the Father, even the Spirit of truth, which proceedeth from the Father, he shall testify of me [not of himself]" (John 15:26). In the next chapter Jesus said, "Howbeit when he, the Spirit of truth, is come, he will guide you into all truth: for he shall not speak of himself; but whatsoever he shall hear, that shall he speak: and he will shew you things to come" (John 16:13). If the Holy Spirit, who is God, does not boast of Himself, why would He permit you to do it?

THE UNBELIEVABLE RESULTS

Paul says, "For we are his workmanship, created in Christ Jesus unto good works, which God hath before ordained that we should walk in them" (Ephesians 2:10). Paul describes the saints in Ephesus as **the providential workmanship**. The image is that of an artist creating a masterpiece. Paul said, "And have put on the new man, which is renewed in knowledge after the image of him that created him" (Colossians 3:10). As believers, we are the creative work of the Master Artist.

When you look at the value of the masterpiece created by God, you must start with **the positional worth** of the art. Yes, it is true that every baptized and born-again believer is now God's workmanship. Yet the masterpiece was created in Christ Jesus. Jesus is the canvas and His blood is the substance used to paint the picture. As God's masterpiece, our value is priceless. This is due to our position in Jesus Christ. It is called "imputed righteousness." When God looks at you, He sees His Son's covering.

The relationship with Christ is confirmed by **the practiced ways**. We are created in Christ Jesus unto *good* works. No, I do not have the right to judge whether a person is saved or not. However, the ways in which a person behaves says a lot about his conversion. Jesus said, "Verily, verily, I say unto you, He that believeth on me, the works that I do shall he do also; and greater works than these shall he do; because I go unto my Father" (John 14:12). Paul said, "Therefore, my beloved brethren, be ye steadfast, unmoveable, always abounding in the work of the Lord, forasmuch as ye know that your labour is not in vain in the Lord" (1 Corinthians 15:58).

The participant's walk should be different from people who have not surrendered their lives to the Lord. Paul said, "That ye might walk worthy of the Lord unto all pleasing, being fruitful in every good work, and increasing in the knowledge of God" (Colossians 1:10). Later on, we will discuss how the believer walks according to the directives given by the Holy Spirit.

The good works are linked to **the provided Word**. How are we to walk? We are to walk according to His Word. The goal of the believer is to operate his life according to the Scriptures. The Bible serves as our road map and guide. It serves as our manual for living. In Ephesians 6, we will see that God's Word is the believer's weapon to fight the enemy.

Let me comment on **the people watching** us. My grandmother used to say, "Sometimes we are the only Bible that some people ever read." As I matured as a believer, I understood what my grandmother meant. When people look at us, they should see the Scriptures in action. They should learn a lot about the Bible from what they see us doing on a daily basis. There are people watching us at all times (especially if we claim to be Christians). They should see evidence of the claim.

I am not dealing with perfect people but **the progressive work** of believers. The truth is that I am a work in progress just like you. God sees the finished product. Guess what? He has started a good work in me and shall see it to completion. Paul said, "Being confident of this very thing, that he which hath begun a good work in you will perform it until the day of Jesus Christ" (Philippians 1:6).

What is the difference between you as a saved brother or sister and other people? The answer is connected to **the preferred worlds**. You don't prefer this world over a relationship with the Lord. Others would rather have this world than anything else. Jesus said, "For what shall it profit a man, if he shall gain the whole world and lose his own soul?" (Mark 8:36). For believers, we desire eternal life in the presence of our Father over anything this world can offer.

Chapter 6

THE BARRIERS REMOVED
EPHESIANS 2:11-18

The Previous Status
The Ancient Categories
The Absent Christ
The Alienated Company
The Assigned Covenant
The Anticipated Continuation
The Accessible Creator
The Awful Conclusion

The Predetermined Solution
The Present Difference
The Profound Dilemma
The Pronounced Death
The Preordained Decision
The Provided Deliverer

The Paid Debt
The Peace Declared
The Partitions Destroyed
The Penalty's Dismissal

The Peace Supplied
The Ruined Fellowship
The Redeemed Flesh
The Recreated Figure
The Received Forgiveness
The Rescue Finalized
The Revealed Freedom
The Reachable Father
The Restored Friendship

IN THE BOOK of Ephesians, Paul desires to show us how great it is for us to be saved. The period between Adam's fall and the death of Christ on the cross would be considered the dark ages for all humanity, including the people of Israel. One day, the Light broke through the darkness and we beheld His glory.

THE PREVIOUS STATUS

Paul says, "Wherefore remember, that ye being in time past Gentiles in the flesh, who are called Uncircumcision by that which is called Circumcision in the flesh made by hands" (Ephesians 2:11). Paul is dealing with **the ancient categories** in this verse. In the ancient world (pre-Calvary) you basically had two categories or classes of people. The Jews took the major ritual of their religion, circumcision, and called themselves by that name, but they classified everyone else as the uncircumcised. The categories were Uncircumcision (Gentiles) or Circumcision (Jews).

Paul says, "That at that time ye were without Christ, being aliens from the commonwealth of Israel, and strangers from the covenants of promise, having no hope, and without God in the world" (Ephesians 2:12). In this verse, Paul deals with **the absent Christ**. As Gentiles, we were without Christ. The Gentiles neither knew nor expected the Messiah (the anointed One of God). There was not a messianic expectation.

Paul described us as **the alienated company** in Ephesians 2:12. Since there was not a messianic hope, we were aliens from God's people (from Israel). As Gentiles, we existed but were not considered citizens of God's nation. Gentiles were merely wanderers in a foreign land. As aliens, they could never file for acceptance into the citizenry that belonged to the people of God.

The assigned covenants were for God's people in the Old Testament. This included all of them (Abrahamic, Mosaic, and Davidic). The covenants did not apply to us originally. We were strangers from the covenants and promises of God. We were not the covenant people of God. We could not go to God based on the promises of the covenant because we were not connected to the agreements outlined in the covenant.

Paul also deals with the absence of **the anticipated continuation.** Gentiles were without hope (see Ephesians 2:12). Gentiles had no hope of life beyond the world or life beyond human history. Once they died, it was considered the end. Life after death was not on their radar. After death, they could not say the words of David recorded in Psalm 23, when he says, "Surely goodness and mercy shall follow me all the days of my life: and I will dwell in the house of the Lord forever" (Psalm 23:6). For the Gentile, life was over on this side.

Paul also deals with **the accessible Creator** for the people of the covenant only in Ephesians 2:12. The children of Israel had limited access to God through the law. Gentiles were without God in the world. This meant that we did not have access to God by any means at all. The Gentile stood alone and had no source of strength to deal with this life.

All of this led to **the awful conclusion** for the Gentile. The cards were stacked against the Gentile according to Ephesians 2:11-12. As a result of all this, Gentiles were destined to die and scheduled to spend eternity separated from God. Without God in our lives on earth, life is a living hell and then we were destined to spend eternity in hell.

THE PREDETERMINED SOLUTION

There was no hope for the Gentile without God stepping in and making the difference. In Ephesians 2:13, Paul deals with **the present difference** from ancient times. Paul says, "But now, in Christ Jesus, ye who sometimes were far off are made nigh by the blood of Christ" (Ephesians 2:13). Here comes the conjunction again. Paul said, "But now . . . " The words *but now* show a powerful contrast taking place. Paul is about to show the difference between the past state and the present status.

One day, one of my sons in the ministry asked, "Since God is rich in mercy and has always had great love for us, why didn't He simply forgive us and save us so that Jesus didn't have to die on the cross?" I shared with him that it was a good question that revealed **the profound dilemma** that only God could address. God has always loved man enough to forgive man. Forgiving humanity has never been the issue for God.

The profound dilemma dealt with **the pronounced death** in the Garden of Eden. God always loved man enough to forgive his transgression and rebellion. That was not the issue. See, there was a problem. The judgment of exile or death had already been pronounced and the Lord's word could not be revoked. God had already declared it and this prevented it from being overturned.

The good news is that God had already worked out a plan. **The preordained decision** to fix the dilemma was made before the dilemma even surfaced. From the beginning, God knew the "Perfect Man" would be the answer to this dilemma. Jesus Christ was the only one qualified. In 2 Corinthians, Paul says, "For he hath made him to be sin for us, *who knew no sin*: that we might be made the righteousness of God in him" (2 Corinthians 5:21, emphasis added).

One day, God sent **the provided Deliverer** to fix the dilemma. In Ephesians 2:13, Paul said, "But now, in Christ Jesus, ye who were sometimes far off are made nigh." In Ephesians 2:12, we were without Christ. In 2:13, we are in Christ Jesus. God provided the Deliverer to end the separation. John says, "For God so loved the world, that he gave his only begotten Son, that whosoever believeth in him should not perish, but have everlasting life" (John 3:16). God provided His only begotten Son to deliver us.

We could not be delivered without Jesus going to the cross. **The paid debt** at Calvary took care of the profound dilemma. It was the blood of Christ that became the acceptable payment (Ephesians 2:13b). Peter says, "Forasmuch as ye know that ye were not redeemed with corruptible things, as silver and gold, from your vain conversation received by tradition from your fathers; But with the precious blood of Christ, as of a lamb without blemish and without spot" (1 Peter 1:18-19).

As a result of Jesus submitting to the will of His Father, we have **the peace declared** by Paul in Ephesians 2:14. We were saved through the actions of the Prince of Peace. Paul says, "For he is our peace, who hath made both one, and hath broken down the middle wall of partition between us" (Ephesians 2:14). Jesus became our peace. This is really a reference to the peace offering of the Old Testament.

The peace offering was a sacrificial offering that was also called a heave and wave offering. This was a bloody offering presented to God. The sacrifice celebrated covering of sin, forgiveness by God, and the restoration of a right and meaningful relationship with God. In Hebrews, the writer says, "How much more shall the blood of Christ, who through the eternal Spirit offered himself without spot to God, purge your conscience from dead works to serve the living God" (Hebrews 9:14).

The shedding of the Savior's blood led to **the partitions destroyed.** In Ephesians 2:14, Paul tells us that Christ has broken down the middle wall of partition between us. This is a picture taken from the temple. The temple was surrounded by a series of courts. Each court had a high wall separating it from the preceding court. As one entered the temple, he entered first the outer Court of the Gentiles (where the buying and selling of animals and exchanging of money for foreign worshippers took place).

Next was the Court of the Women. The next one was the Court of the Israelites. This is where the whole congregation gathered on the great feast days and where sacrifices were handed over to the priests. The Court of the Priests was next. It was considered sacred and was only accessible to the services of the priests. Finally, within the heart of the temple stood the Holy of Holies (or the Most Holy Place) where the very presence of God was to dwell. Only the High Priest could enter the Holy Place and he could only enter once a year—at the great Passover Feast.

The actions of Jesus led to **the penalty's dismissal.** Paul says, "Having abolished in his flesh the enmity, even the law of commandments contained in ordinances; for to make in himself of twain one new man, so making peace" (Ephesians 2:15). Christ brought peace by wiping out the enmity of the law against us. Before Christ, man had to approach God through law. However, man discovered something: The law did not make him acceptable to God. As a matter of fact, it condemned him and showed him how far away from God he really was—totally depraved. Each time he broke the law, the law cried out "guilty" and pronounced the penalty of being imperfect and unworthy and unacceptable to God.

Man discovered that the law was against him—at enmity with him. But now Christ has done away with the enmity and condemnation of the law. Jesus said, "Think not that I am come to destroy the law, or the prophets: I am not come to destroy, but to fulfil" (Matthew 5:17). In Galatians, Paul said, "Christ hath redeemed us from the curse of the law, being made a curse for us: for it is written, Cursed is every one that hangeth on a tree" (Galatians 3:13).

THE PEACE SUPPLIED

Sin led to **the ruined fellowship** between God and man. Adam and Eve were banned from God's presence immediately after they sinned. God could not permit the sinful nature of humanity to remain in His perfect paradise. God fixed the problem by sending the Perfect Person from paradise into the sinful world where sinners resided.

It took **the Redeemer's flesh** to remedy the problem. Jesus Christ, in His flesh, abolished the enmity (see Ephesians 2:15a). The reason His death was acceptable and He qualified as Redeemer is due to the fact that there was no sin connected to His flesh. If Jesus had committed one sin on earth, it would have disqualified Him from serving as our Redeemer. His perfection paved the way to our pardon. In Romans 8:3, Paul says, "For what the law could not do, in that it was weak through the flesh, God sending his own Son in the likeness of sinful flesh, and for sin, condemned sin in the flesh."

The obedience of Jesus Christ produced **the recreated figure**. In Ephesians 2:15, Paul says Jesus did what He did "to make in himself of twain one new man, so making peace." It was no longer Jew and Gentile. He took the Jew and Gentile and made one new figure. It's all about the DNA (Divine Nature Attached). In the book of Galatians, Paul describes this divine fusion when he says, 'There is neither Jew nor Greek, there is neither bond or free, there is neither male nor female: for ye are all one in Christ Jesus" (Galatians 3:28).

As noted in the introduction, redemption and reconciliation are the primary messages presented in the Pauline Epistles. At the end of Ephesians 2:15, the phrase "so making peace" deals with the two becoming one by His peace offering. The phrase "making peace" deals with **the received forgiveness**. Jesus Christ did us a favor so that we would be forgiven. He became the required offering for us.

Next we have **the rescue finalized**. Paul said, "And that he might reconcile both unto God in one body by the cross, having slain the enmity thereby" (Ephesians 2:16). Look at how Jesus reconciled both (Jew and Gentile) in one body. It was by the cross. The rescue and reconciliation was finalized when Jesus said, "It is finished" while hanging on the cross. By the way, the Easter act of God must be believed in order for us to be saved but the resurrection did not pave the way for us to be saved. It was the blood and the cross that did it. In Colossians, Paul says, "And, having made peace through the blood of his cross, by him to reconcile all things unto himself; by him, I say, whether they be things in earth, or things in heaven" (Colossians 1:20).

In Ephesians 2:17, we are told that Jesus Christ preached peace to the Gentile (those that were afar off) and the Jew (them that were nigh). This message of peace dealt with **the revealed freedom** we have through Jesus Christ. The door to the kingdom was reopened for man to freely enter. The sins of Adam locked the door of the kingdom, which prevented us from getting to God. The death of Jesus unlocked the door for us to freely return. In Galatians, Paul speaks of this freedom when he says, "For, brethren, ye have been called unto liberty; only use not liberty for an occasion to the flesh, but by love serve one another" (Galatians 5:13).

As a result of the death, burial, and resurrection of Jesus Christ, we now have access to **the reachable Father.** We can call on Him and expect Him to answer because we belong to Him. We are our heavenly Father's children and we have been given access to Him at all times. Paul said, "For through him we both have access by one Spirit unto the Father" (Ephesians 2:18). Once again, we see the triune God in this verse. By receiving the Son, we have access to the Father by His Spirit.

In essence, sin led to the fallout, but the shedding of blood led to **the restored friendship.** The actions of Jesus changed the ancient categories mentioned earlier to something better than we could ever imagine. When Jesus was on earth with His disciples, He stopped calling His disciples servants and called them friends. He said, "Greater love hath no man than this, that a man lay down his life for his friends. Ye are my friends, if ye do whatsoever I command you. Henceforth I call you not servants; for the servant knoweth not what his lord doeth: but I have called you friends; for all things that I have heard of my Father I have made known unto you" (John 15:13-15).

Chapter 7

THE HOUSE THAT GOD BUILT

EPHESIANS 2:19-22

The Beautiful Family
The Past Condition
The People Chosen
The Permanent Citizenship
The Planted Church
The Privileged Children
The Personal Commitment

The Building's Founder
The Construction Project
The Cornerstone Placed
The Conversion Process

The Connected Pieces
The Concrete Poured

The Big Facility
The Living Stone
The Life Support
The Lifestyle Shift
The Large Structure
The Light Shining
The League Saved
The Local Sanctuary
The Leader Supplied

AFTER THE DEATH of Jesus, the construction of the house of God started. Every born-again believer is an important part of the household of faith. In Ephesians 2:19-22, Paul shows us how the house was constructed by our heavenly Father.

THE BEAUTIFUL FAMILY

In the first few chapters of Ephesians, Paul is basically going over the same information. He says, "Now therefore ye are no more strangers and foreigners, but fellow citizens with the saints, and of the household of God" (Ephesians 2:19). He desires the believer to understand the basic message of the Gospel. Once again, he deals with **the past condition**. Paul said, "Now therefore ye are no more strangers and foreigners" (2:19a). The word *stranger* means an outsider or a person who does not belong. The word *foreigner* means an alien, a migrant, an exile. In the past, we had no relationship and no fellowship with God. We had no rights to citizenship in His kingdom.

As a result of Jesus serving as the sacrificial Lamb, we are now **the people chosen** by God. We are now people selected and set apart (saints) by God to be joint heirs with Christ. He selected and sanctified us. Jesus said, "Ye have not chosen me, but I have chosen you, and ordained you, that ye should go and bring forth fruit, and that your fruit should remain" (John 15:16).

Jesus is the reason for **the permanent citizenship** of people who were once considered strangers. We are now fellow-citizens. When a foreigner came to a country, he was required to seek permission for a temporary visit. God did not permit us to simply visit; He allowed us to become citizens with the saints. Yes, in the past, the request for citizenship was denied. Now the citizenship request is honored through the shed blood of Jesus Christ.

The planted church occurred when Jesus came and died for the sins of the world. When Jesus declared from the cross that it was finished, He was dealing with the foundation of the church being established. All believers comprise the household of God. Jesus said, "Upon this rock I will build my church; and the gates of hell shall not prevail against it" (Matthew 16:18). Jesus Christ fully understood that His mission was to build the church.

Paul reminds us that we have become **the privileged children** of the Father. The term *household* deals with the privilege of adoption given to all believers. We have been adopted as children of God. We now live in the same house with God and the rest of the family. In Romans, Paul says, "For ye have not received the spirit of bondage again to fear; but ye have received the Spirit of adoption, whereby we cry, Abba, Father. The Spirit itself beareth witness with our spirit, that we are the children of God: and if children, then heirs; heirs of God, and joint-heirs with Christ; if so be that we suffer with him, that we may be also glorified together" (Romans 8:15-17). We were adopted into the family with all rights and privileges granted to us.

The term *household* also points to those who have made **the personal commitment** to serve. Every person of the household of God has duties to perform, some service to render for the sake of the family. We have too many family members not doing their part in the house. We are to love, care, provide for, and teach each other. In John, Jesus said, "I then, your Lord and Master, have washed your feet; ye also ought to wash one another's feet" (John 13:14).

THE BUILDING'S FOUNDER

Paul says, "And are built upon the foundation of the apostles and prophets, Jesus Christ himself being the chief corner stone" (Ephesians 2:20). The church is pictured as God's building. **The construction project** involves several phases. As we shall see in this section of Ephesians, all born-again believers are building stones used to construct this building of God. I attended a dedication service a few years ago following the completion of a new sanctuary in Arkansas. In the parking lot, they had a section called "the path to the promise" with beautiful bricks with the names of every member of the church on the bricks. In a real sense, Paul is telling us that every brick in God's building has the name of a believer on it because we are His stones.

The construction project starts with **the Cornerstone placed**. Jesus Christ Himself is the chief cornerstone. Since Jesus is the chief cornerstone, if He is removed, the building will collapse: no Christ, no church. Christ holds everything within the church together. He is the Head of the church and without Him, the church would not exist.

How did we become God's stones? It took **the conversion process** occurring in our lives. The only way for us to be used in this construction project is to be converted. We have to look to the chief cornerstone for this to take place. The writer of Hebrews says, "Looking unto Jesus the author and finisher of our faith; who for the joy that was set before him endured the cross, despising the shame, and is set down at the right hand of the throne of God" (Hebrews 12:2). Our faith starts and ends with Jesus.

The cornerstone is also the supportive stone. After the cornerstone is placed, **the connected stones** are aligned with it. All other stones are placed upon it and held up by it. The cornerstone is the preeminent stone in position and power. Jesus Christ is the support and power by which the whole building stands. The cornerstone is also known as the "directional stone." It is used to line up the whole building and all the other stones. The pattern flows from the cornerstone.

Jesus is the chief cornerstone and God uses Him to give direction to all the other stones. Peter says, "Wherefore also it is contained in the scripture, Behold, I lay in Zion a chief cornerstone, elect, precious: and he that believeth on him shall not be confounded. Unto you therefore which believe he is precious: but unto them which are disobedient, the stone which the builders disallowed, the same is made the head of the corner" (1 Peter 2:6-7).

All of the points previously mentioned must be built on a solid foundation. Paul deals with **the concrete poured** for the building's foundation. We are built upon the foundation laid by the testimonies of the apostles and prophets. The apostles and prophets are not the foundation of the building. Their testimonies represent the foundation laid. Therefore, the Word of God is the foundation on which the church is laid.

In Romans Paul says, "For I am not ashamed of the gospel of Christ: for it is the power of God *unto salvation* to everyone that believeth: to the Jew first, and also to the Greek" (Romans 1:16, emphasis added). He also says, "But what saith it? The word is nigh thee, even in thy mouth, and in thy heart: that is, the word of faith, which we preach; that if thou shall confess with thy mouth the Lord Jesus, and shalt believe in thine heart that God hath raised him from the dead, thou shalt be saved" (Romans 10:8-9).

THE BIG FACILITY

The church is pictured as a growing organism connected to the living stone. Paul says, "In whom all the building fitly framed together groweth unto an holy temple in the Lord: In whom ye also are builded together for an habitation of God through the Spirit" (Ephesians 2:21-22). The word *grow* is a biological term that doesn't seem to go with a construction project, but it does from a spiritual perspective. Why? The chief stone is also called a living stone that produces lively stones. Peter says, "To whom coming, as unto a living stone, disallowed indeed of men, but chosen of God, and precious, Ye also, as lively stones are built up a spiritual house, an holy priesthood, to offer up spiritual sacrifices, acceptable to God by Jesus Christ" (1 Peter 2:4-5).

The life support comes from the living stone. Since Christ is the living stone, our life is supported by Him. Before Christ, we were dead in trespasses and sins. In Christ, we are now on spiritual life support. It is through Him that we live, move, and have our being. Jesus said, "The thief cometh not, but for to steal, and to kill, and to destroy: I am come that they may have life, and that they might have it more abundantly" (John 10:10).

As a result of our souls being linked to the giver of life, we have the power to do all things. Paul says, "I can do all things through Christ which strengtheneth me" (Philippians 4:13). If we were not connected to Him, we could do nothing. Jesus said, "I am the vine, ye are the branches: He that abideth in me, and I in him, the same bringeth forth much fruit; for without me ye can do nothing" (John 15:5).

We are not only linked but the text informs us that we are growing unto a holy temple in the Lord (2:21b). **The lifestyle shift** occurs because of the connection to Christ. The word *growth* points to maturity. If you are presently and properly connected to Christ, spiritual growth should be taking place. When we grow in Christ, we don't look the same as we did when we first started off. Our spiritual development is like our physical development. We start off as babes in Christ on milk. As we develop, we soon move from milk to meat. As a result, we stop acting like babes in Christ.

The growth also deals with **the large structure** that now exists and it continues to grow in size. The term *growth* also deals with the building getting bigger or larger. Since the Savior was resurrected, the church has continued to grow in size. Every time a person is saved, a new brother or sister is added to the family.

We need **the light shining** in the house of God at all times. There must be a light shining in the life of the believer to attract people. Jesus is the light that shines in me. Jesus said, "Let your light so shine before men, that they may see your good works, and glorify your Father which is in heaven" (Matthew 5:16). As we shine for Christ, we are witnesses to the world about the saving power of Jesus Christ. As a result, the building continues to grow in size. Jesus said, "And I, if I be lifted up from the earth; will draw all men unto me" (John 12:32).

Next let me deal with **the league saved**. One Sunday out of each month at the church where I serve as pastor, we have the children, youth, and adults in the main auditorium. Normally, the children worship upstairs and the youth worship in the chapel. One Sunday, I heard a child ask her mom an interesting question as they entered the building. She said, "Mom, are we all going to be in the big church today?"

Paul says, "In whom *all the building* fitly framed together groweth unto an holy temple in the Lord" (Ephesians 2:21, emphasis added). A league is an association of nations comprising one unit that promotes common interests. The church is pictured as a worldwide temple. There are times when we seemingly forget about "the big church" that exists in this world. Paul used the word *all* in Ephesians 2:21 to let us know that all believers make up the holy temple of God. People from all generations across the globe are a part of this spiritual league.

Paul not only addresses the church worldwide, he also deals with **the local sanctuary** or church. When he uses the word *you* (*ye*) in Ephesians 2:22, he is referring to the Ephesian church in particular. Each local congregation or church is pictured as a building structured for God's purpose and power. Each local temple is a part of the big facility. The local church exists for the purpose of providing a habitation, a home for the presence of God. God needs a habitation in every part of the world. Therefore, He resides in your life as His habitation.

Look at **the Leader supplied** according to Ephesians 2:22. Paul says, "In whom ye also are builded together for an habitation of God through the Spirit." Notice, we are the home or habitation of God through the Spirit. The Holy Spirit has been supplied to every believer. The Holy Spirit dwells within the church to accomplish several things.

- The Holy Spirit seals us (Ephesians 1:13-14). We have the glorious guarantee of spending eternity in heaven (Romans 8:16).

- The Holy Spirit comforts us (John 14:17-18).
- The Holy Spirit teaches us (John 14:26).
- The Holy Spirit guides us (John 16:13).
- The Holy Spirit empowers us (Acts 1:8).
- The Holy Spirit helps us and intercedes for us (Romans 8:26-27).
- The Holy Spirit leads us (Romans 8:14).
- The Holy Spirit liberates us (2 Corinthians 3:17).
- The Holy Spirit unites us (1 Corinthians 12:13-14).
- The Holy Spirit strengthens us (Ephesians 3:16).

Chapter 8

A CHARGE TO KEEP I HAVE
EPHESIANS 3:1-13

The Called Apostle
The Prisoner Speaks
The Proud Slave
The Permitted Suffering
The Picked Steward
The Privileged Servant
The People Selected
The Precious Savior

The Church Age
The Revelation Received
The Revealer's Release
The Released Rebels
The Ransom Required

The Relationship Rights
The Religious Rituals

The Commissioned Ambassador
The Made Minister
The Metamorphic Miracle
The Missing Merit
The Mysterious Message
The Mandated Mission
The Majestic Marveling
The Marvelous Membership
The Magnificent Mediator
The Miserable Moments

AS A BOY attending the Zion Hill Baptist Church in Camden, Arkansas, I used to hear my dad leading the devotional service on Sunday mornings. One of his favorite hymns was entitled, "A Charge to Keep I Have." The words of the first stanza went something like this:

A charge to keep I have
A God to glorify
A never-dying soul to save
Fitted for the sky

In chapter three of Ephesians, Paul begins a new division. In this first section of the new division, Paul deals with his call and charge from Christ for the church.

THE CALLED APOSTLE

Once again, **the prisoner speaks**. Paul says, "For this cause I Paul, the prisoner of Jesus Christ for you Gentiles" (Ephesians 3:1). Let me deal with the dual meaning of the term *prisoner* in this verse. First of all, he is speaking literally because he is imprisoned in Rome as he pens these words. He is on lockdown. He is awaiting a court date.

As a prisoner of Jesus Christ, Paul is identifying himself as **the proud slave** of his Master, Jesus Christ. He is also speaking figuratively from a spiritual perspective. He is a proud slave or prisoner of Jesus Christ. Being enslaved to Christ was something to be proud of. Before Christ, he was in the chains of the enemy like all of us. God loosed his shackles and set him free.

As a bondservant of Jesus Christ, he ended up in prison. In other words, as a prisoner of the Lord, he ended up becoming a prisoner in the land. This informs the reader of **the permitted suffering** connected to serving the Lord. Jesus informed Ananias of the suffering Paul would encounter as His servant. In Acts 9:16, Jesus says, "For I will shew him how great things he must suffer for my name's sake."

In Ephesians 3:2, he uses the word *dispensation* to drive home the same point. He is informing the reader that he is **the picked steward** of Jesus Christ. He says, "If ye have heard of the dispensation of the grace of God which is given me to you-ward"

(Ephesians 3:2). The word *dispensation* means stewardship, management, administration. Paul was given the duty to oversee and administer the grace of God to the world. In 1 Corinthians 4:1-2, Paul said, "Let a man so account of us, as of the ministers of Christ, and stewards of the mysteries of God. Moreover it is required in stewards, that a man be found faithful."

As a slave and steward suffering for the Savior, he views himself as **the privileged servant** of the Lord. It is through the dispensation *of the grace of God.* In Ephesians 3:7, he calls it the gift of the grace of God. In one of Paul's letters to Timothy, he says, "According to the glorious gospel of the blessed God, which was committed to my trust. And I thank Christ Jesus our Lord, who hath enabled me, for that he counted me faithful, putting me into the ministry" (1 Timothy 1:11-12). We should consider it a blessed privilege to serve the Lord.

Look at **the people selected** to be blessed by the ministry of Paul. He says, "If ye have heard of the dispensation of the grace of God, which is given me to you-ward" (Ephesians 3:2). The term *you-ward* is a reference to the Gentiles mentioned in verse one. Paul was picked specifically to preach the gospel to the Gentiles and Jews. Let's look at the message God gave Ananias in Damascus regarding Paul from the book of Acts. Luke says, "But the Lord said unto him, Go thy way: for he is a chosen vessel unto me, to bear my name before the Gentiles, and kings, and the children of Israel" (Acts 9:15). The order is intentional. Paul's ministry focused primarily on the Gentiles. Yes, he ministered to all, but the Gentiles served as his primary target.

According to Ephesians 3:4, Paul said he was called and chosen to preach the "mystery of Christ" to them. He was the picked servant and steward to unveil the mystery of Christ to them. The unveiled mystery is about **the precious Savior** and Him alone. Paul would have been considered an Old Testament scholar of his day. When he was converted, he continued to expound on the Old Testament when he taught others. He simply showed how everything in the Old Testament pointed to the New Testament and Jesus Christ.

THE CHURCH AGE

The revelation received by Paul had already been shared with the believers in Ephesus. Paul said, "How that by revelation he made known unto me the mystery (as I wrote afore in few words; Whereby when ye read, ye may understand my knowledge in the mystery of Christ)" (Ephesians 3:3-4). It is called "the mystery of Christ." The word *mystery* (*musterion*) is defined in these verses. As mentioned earlier, in the Bible a mystery is not some mysterious or difficult thing to understand. It is a truth that has been locked up in God's plan for ages until He was ready to reveal it to man.

When the time came, He unlocked the treasure or truth and opened it up to man. It was some truth that had to be revealed by God for man to know it. As Ephesians 3:5 says: "In other ages it was not made known to the sons of men" (author paraphrase). According to verse nine, the mystery, from the beginning of the world has been hid in God. It was for an appointed time. Yes, there were hints of the mystery given in the Old Testament, but the mystery was not made known until the New Testament period came. This is when Jesus, the One with the mystery, came and dwelt among us.

The mystery was received following **the Revealer's release**. Paul says, "Which in other ages was not made known unto the sons of men, as it is now revealed unto his holy apostles and prophets by the Spirit" (Ephesians 3:5). Paul describes the Holy Spirit as the revealer of the revelation in 1 Corinthians. He says, "But God hath revealed them unto us by his Spirit: for the Spirit searcheth all things, yea, the deep things of God" (1 Corinthians 2:10).

One of the key assignments given to the Holy Spirit is to reveal truth during the church age. Jesus declared this in the

Gospel of John. Jesus says, "Howbeit when he, the Spirit of truth, is come, he will guide you into all truth: for he shall not speak of himself; but whatsoever he shall hear, that shall he speak: and he will shew you things to come. He shall glorify me: for he shall receive of mine, and shall shew it unto you" (John 16:13-14).

The revealed truth led to **the released rebels.** Check out what the revealer made known in Ephesians 3:6. He said, "That the Gentile should be fellow heirs, and of the same body, and partakers of his promise in Christ by the gospel." Let's start at the end of this verse this time. The Gentile was released "in Christ by the gospel." He is dealing with the Gentiles coming to know Christ by the gospel. Before being "in Christ," we were all rebels ruled by Satan. Jesus came and rescued us from our rebellious state. In Romans 6:17, Paul said, "But God be thanked, that ye were the servants of sin, but ye have obeyed from the heart that form of doctrine which was delivered you." Before the gospel was delivered to us, we were servants of sin doomed to die.

Don't forget about **the ransom required** for the rescue. How did He rescue us? He did it by paying the required ransom (death on the cross). Jesus paid the price by dying for us. As a result of the ransom paid, no person is beyond the reach of the Redeemer. Salvation is available for any and all sinners willing to be saved. Paul said, "For whosoever shall call upon the name of the Lord shall be saved" (Romans 10:13).

As a result of being rescued and redeemed, **the relationship rights** were granted to all believers, including Gentiles. He said, "That *the Gentiles should be fellowheirs,* and of the same body, and partakers of his promise in Christ by the gospel" (Ephesians 3:6, emphasis added). As a result of being in Christ, we are now fellow heirs and in the same body and partakers of the promise as the Jew. We have all the rights and privileges as a result of being in Christ.

We received these rights without having to engage in **the religious rituals** of the Jews. No circumcision is required. You don't have to stop by a farm to purchase an animal to sacrifice at the altar when you come to the Lord's house. Jesus became the ultimate and only sacrifice acceptable to the Lord. As a result of Jesus serving as the acceptable sacrifice, you have become a living sacrifice in Jesus Christ.

THE COMMISSIONED AMBASSADOR

Paul identifies himself as **the minister made** by God. Paul said, "Whereof I was made a minister, according to the gift of the grace of God given unto me by the effectual working of his power" (Ephesians 3:7). The word *made* means "to create." The clergy should be called and chosen by the Creator. You cannot do this on your own. In Colossians 1:25, he said, "Whereof I am made a minister, according to the dispensation of God which is given to me *for you*, to fulfil the word of God" (emphasis added).

Paul came with a lot of baggage but God made him a minister. **The metamorphic miracle** took place by the hand of God. God creates masterpieces from messes. In 1 Corinthians, Paul says, "For I am the least of the apostles, that am not meet to be called an apostle, because I persecuted the church of God. But by the grace of God I am what I am . . ." (1 Corinthians 15:9-10a). Paul labeled himself as the chief among sinners. He says, "This is a faithful saying, and worthy of acceptance, that Christ Jesus came into the world to save sinners; of whom I am chief" (1 Timothy 1:15). It is nothing short of a miracle to see how God can transform a wretched person from Tarsus or Arkansas and mold him into a minister.

Look at **the missing merit** in Paul's message. Paul said, "Unto me, who am less than the least of all saints, is this grace given . . ." (Ephesians 3:8a). There was no merit, no worth, no value within Paul that qualified him to preach the gospel. God's selection is never based on merit. As a matter of fact, the only one qualified to do this is the one who realizes that he is unqualified. Paul says,

"For though I preach the gospel, I have nothing to glory of: for necessity is laid upon me: yea, woe is unto me, if I preach not the gospel" (1 Corinthians 9:16).

Paul said, "That I should preach among the Gentiles the unsearchable riches of Christ; And to make all men see what is the fellowship of the mystery, which from the beginning of the world hath been hid in God, who created all things by Jesus Christ" (Ephesians 3:8-9). The "unsearchable riches of Christ" is **the mysterious message**. The word *unsearchable* means untrackable by human means. It is that treasure in earthen vessels that can only be discovered in Christ.

Look at **the mandated mission** in Ephesians 3:9. Paul said, "And to make all men see what is the fellowship of the mystery, which from the beginning of the world hath been hid in God, who created all things by Jesus Christ." Paul is basically saying, "My mission is to get the message out to every man, woman, boy, or girl (make all men see)." This does not mean that all men will accept the message, but the mandated mission is to make sure all men have the gospel presented to them.

In Ephesians 3:10-11, Paul deals with what I want to call **the majestic marveling**. Paul says, "To the intent that now unto the principalities and powers in heavenly places might be known by the church the manifold wisdom of God, According to the eternal purpose which is purposed in Christ Jesus our Lord." The revealed mystery of Christ has profoundly affected heavenly beings. It causes them to stand in stark amazement at what God is doing in the church through Christ. Don't forget that the mystery was hid in God from the beginning of time. This means that heavenly beings didn't know the mystery.

There is some debate by theologians as to which principalities and powers in heavenly places Paul is referring to in Ephesians 3:10. There are those who believe they are the hostile angels in the unseen world. They believe they are the fallen ones who help Satan rule this planet. Others believe that the verse is referring to the angelic host of God. Then you have me. I believe all principalities and powers in heavenly places witness a mind-blowing experience as they see what Christ is doing through His church.

Devils tremble and angels rejoice over Christ's power. Paul says, "Wherefore God also hath highly exalted him, and given him a name which is above every name: That at the name of Jesus every knee should bow, of things in heaven, and things in earth, and things under the earth: And that every tongue should confess that Jesus Christ is Lord, to the glory of God the Father" (Philippians 2:9-11). Before it is all over, everyone will marvel over His majesty.

Let's talk about **the marvelous membership** made possible by the death, burial, and resurrection of Jesus Christ. Membership has its privileges. After the mystery is revealed and received, the believer has access to the presence of God. We can boldly reach out to God by faith. It is the mature member who realizes what Paul says in Ephesians 3:12: "In whom we have boldness and access with confidence by the faith of him." We have confident assurance through faith that we can access the throne of God at all times. It is like my sons when they come to the house. They don't have to ring the doorbell; they have keys to unlock the door and come in. We have the keys to enter our heavenly Father's house.

Jesus is presented as **the magnificent Mediator** who gives us access to the Father. Paul said, "In whom we have boldness and access with confidence *by the faith of him*" (Ephesians 3:12, emphasis added). It is by faith "of him" that we have this bold confidence to access the throne of God. This is why we pray "in the name of Jesus." There is no other way to gain access. We cannot gain access by our worth or works but by Him.

I love how Paul often includes a verse or two in his writings to remind us of **the miserable moments** connected to ministry. In Ephesians 3:13, Paul said, "Wherefore I desire that ye faint not at my tribulations for you, which is your glory." Isn't it interesting that Paul brings up the subject of tribulation after telling us we can boldly approach the throne of God with confidence? This should allow us to see that prayer does not always prevent problems from coming into our lives. Instead of focusing on the gloom resulting from the tribulation, Paul addresses the glory. In Ephesians 3:13, Paul is basically reflecting on his imprisonment and all of the suffering encountered and saying, "It's all worth it." It was worth it because many souls were added to the kingdom.

One night, while I was watching the local news, there was a report shared about a boy falling in a well. The reporter was interviewing the man who pulled a boy out of a well that he had fallen in a few days ago. The boy ended up having emergency surgery as a result of a major head injury. They had to remove fluid from his brain. In the news story, they showed the boy out of the hospital playing around in the yard as they interviewed the neighbor who saved him. They asked the man to take them through the moment when he rescued the boy.

He explained how he tied some long straps and climbed down to the boy. He was bruised and battered as he went down and eventually covered with water. Later the paramedics arrived to help him pull the boy out. The reporter said, "You went through a lot to save the boy." He said, "I didn't mind getting bruised and soaked just to see him alive and well!" Paul is saying the same thing. It's worth the struggle to see the glory and good that comes from sharing the gospel.

Chapter 9

BEYOND CONVERSION
EPHESIANS 3:14-21

THE RIGHTEOUS PATH

PAUL SAID, "FOR this cause I bow my knees unto the Father of our Lord Jesus Christ" (Ephesians 3:14). We have **the servant praying**. The work of Christ in the life of the believer requires prayer. Paul made it clear to the new converts in Ephesus that he

81

was praying for them and the church at large. He says, "For this cause I bow my knees. . . . " This prayer drove Paul to his knees.

Look at **the specific purpose** for his praying. He says, "For this cause I bow my knees." What is "this cause" referenced in the verse? It deals with the redemption provided to the Gentiles already discussed from Ephesians 1 to this point in the passage. Paul is referring back to the great salvation and birth of the church. God is building the body of believers (the church) and this work must be completed. Therefore, Paul is praying specifically for this to happen.

He is bowing his knees "unto the Father of our Lord Jesus Christ of whom the whole family in heaven and earth is named" (Ephesians 3:14b-15). Paul again describes God as the Father of our Lord Jesus Christ in this verse. He places emphasis on **the Savior's Parent** to show us how we are now members of the family. He is praying to the One who made it all possible. He is praying through the One who made access possible. He is praying to the only living and true God, who is the Father of all believers who have ever believed and trusted His promise, both past and present. We understand how the ones present and in the future are saved but what about those in the past who died before Christ came? The blood reaches back to those who looked for the promise.

He is also praying to the Father through the Son for them because he knew **the saints' potential** to accomplish a lot for the kingdom. They would be responsible for leading others into the kingdom or family of God. These new converts had barely tapped the surface of their potential in Christ. Paul wanted them to know that conversion was the starting point and not the destination or finish line. They were packed with untapped potential. God wanted to use them. God had equipped them with all the necessary tools to turn the world upside down for the kingdom.

He prayed for **the strengthening process** to take over. He prayed that God would "grant them according to the riches of his glory, to be strengthened with might" (Ephesians 3:16a). The first request is for strength and power. The word *strengthen* means to be made strong, tough, enduring. It means to have energy to act, endure, or resist. The word *might* means power.

In Colossians, he says, "Strengthened with all might, according to his glorious power, unto all patience and longsuffering with joyfulness" (Colossians 1:11). This strength and power cause us to be patient and longsuffering. While we are waiting, we still have joy! Isaiah said, "But they that wait upon the Lord shall renew their strength; they shall mount up with wings as eagles; they shall run, and not be weary; and they shall walk, and not faint" (Isaiah 40:31).

He also prayed for **the Spirit's power** to prevail. He says, "To be strengthened with might by his Spirit in the inner man" (Ephesians 3:16b). The source of the strength and might is the Holy Spirit of God. John said, "Ye are of God, little children, and have overcome them: because greater is he that is in you, than he that is in the world" (1 John 4:4). We cannot do anything for the kingdom of God without assistance from the Holy Spirit. As a matter of fact, Jesus made this point clear before he returned to His Father in heaven. Before departing, He said, "But ye shall receive power, after that the Holy Ghost is come upon you: and ye shall be witnesses unto me both in Jerusalem, and in all Judaea, and in Samaria, and unto the uttermost part of the earth" (Acts 1:8).

Paul prayed that we would be strengthened with might by His Spirit in the inner man (3:16c). The "inner man" is **the spiritual part** of your design. The outward man is the "earthen vessel," the mortal flesh, and the earthly house. The inner man is the deepest part of your being. It is the spirit of man that has been born again. It is the spirit of man that was dead in trespasses and sins until it was quickened and made alive by Christ. This is the part Paul spoke of in 2 Corinthians 4:16 when he said, "For which cause we faint not; but though our outward man perish, yet the inward man is renewed day by day."

THE RADIATING PRESENCE

He is praying that Christ will dwell in our hearts. Paul says, "That Christ may dwell in your hearts by faith" (Ephesians 3:17). Christ is **the dwelling force** that causes us to walk in victory. The request is for Christ to dwell, that is, rule and reign in our hearts. The word *dwell* means a permanent not a temporary dwelling. It means to take up permanent residence: to live in a home; to enter, unpack, settle down, and be at home. Paul is not praying for Christ to enter the hearts and lives of believers; Christ is already in hearts and lives. What is Paul praying for? He is praying that we will allow Jesus to unpack, settle down, and be at home in our hearts.

In John, Jesus said, "I in them, and thou in me, that they may be made perfect in one; and that the world may know that thou has sent me, and has loved them, as thou has loved me" (John 17:23). In Galatians, Paul says, "I am crucified with Christ: nevertheless I live; yet not I, but Christ liveth in me: and the life which I now live in the flesh I live by faith of the Son of God, who loved me, and gave himself for me" (Galatians 2:20).

He dwells in the heart by faith. He is not dealing with "saving" faith here. They had been converted already. He is dealing with **the developing faith** or maturing faith that comes as we grow. The idea is that the heart is the home of God. The more of God we allow in our hearts the more the believer is able to rise above "shallow" faith. It leads a believer into "deep water" faith.

As saints grow, **the disciples' fruit** begins to ripen. Paul said, "That ye, being rooted and grounded in love . . . " (Ephesians 3:17b). The fruit of love is produced when this dwelling force and developing faith exists. The authenticating evidence of discipleship is seen when we are rooted and grounded in love. Jesus said, "A new commandment I give unto you, that ye love one another; as I have loved you, that ye also love one another. By this shall all men know that you are my disciples, if ye have love one to another" (John 13:34-35). In Galatians, Paul says, "But the fruit of the Spirit is love, joy, peace, longsuffering, gentleness, goodness, faith, 23 meekness, temperance: against such there is no law" (Galatians 5:22-23).

Spiritual growth deals with **the deepened familiarity** with spiritual things. Paul wanted the believers in Ephesus to be "able to comprehend with all saints, what is the breadth, and length, and depth, and height" of what God is doing for His children (see Ephesians 3:18). This faith and love will help us comprehend or become more familiar with the things that matter most. We become more and more familiar but never fully comprehend what God has done, is doing, and will do. It cannot be measured. However, we must seek to comprehend the breadth and length and depth and height of what God does for us and the church. Paul is dealing with the one seeking to comprehend the greatness of salvation. The more you comprehend, the more you apply to your daily walk. Your comprehension should cause you to become more committed to Him.

Paul deals with **the devotee's focus** when he says, "And to know the love of Christ, which passeth knowledge. . . . " On a daily basis, we should focus more and more on the love of Christ (which surpasses knowledge). It is utterly impossible to grasp the love of Christ fully but we should seek to learn more and more of His love. In John, Jesus said, "If a man love me, he will keep my words: and my Father will love him, and we will come unto him, and make our abode with him" (John 14:23). There is no way to measure the amount of love God has for us, but our obedience will cause the love of God to take over in our lives.

Paul said, "And to know the love of Christ, which passeth knowledge, that ye might be filled with the fulness of God"

(Ephesians 3:19). The "fullness of God" deals with **the different functions** of the Godhead. The ultimate goal is to be filled with all the fullness of God. When we were converted, we received the divine package, the fullness of God. Each person of the Godhead has a different function within the lives of all believers. Earlier Paul told us that the believer is to pray to be strengthened by the Holy Spirit and to have Christ dwell within and control his heart (see Ephesians 3:16-17). Now the believer is to pray for all the fullness of God Himself. It basically means for the triune God to have His way in our lives.

THE REJOICING PERIOD

Paul has much more to say to the Ephesians in this letter but **the excited servant** has a personal praise period at the end of Ephesians 3. He says, "Now unto him that is able to do exceeding abundantly above all that we ask or think, according to the power that worketh in us" (Ephesians 3:20). Paul has to pause to pay homage to the Lord, who is responsible for all of these incredible things happening in the life of believers. You can almost see him looking toward heaven as he starts speaking in Ephesians 3:20. He says, "Now, unto him. . . . " It is similar to Jude's message when he says, "Now unto him that is able to keep you from falling, and to present you faultless before the presence of his glory with exceeding joy" (Jude 24).

Paul had faith and knew God could give him the desires of his heart. He mentions this in Romans, when he says, "And being fully persuaded that, what he had promised, he was able also to perform" (Romans 4:21). Yet in this passage, he is looking at God's ability to do much more. He is rejoicing because **the expectations surpassed** his desires. To do "exceedingly" means to surpass. God is able to easily surpass our expectations.

The experienced spillover has occurred in the life of every believer. The word *abundantly* means to create an overflow. It carries the idea of a cup overflowing due to being filled to the brim but the substance continues to pour. It is similar to what David experienced when he said, "Thou anointest my head with oil; my cup runneth over" (Psalm 23:5). I thought about my childhood days at the breakfast table for a moment. The experienced spillover is like my mom pouring my dad a cup of coffee and she often poured so much that it spilled over into the saucer underneath.

There is **the extra stuff** that comes as a result of the overflow. This is similar to abundance but the word goes a little further. You abundantly receive the substance desired but He goes above and beyond by giving you extra stuff. It is a like a fountain that overflows (abundantly) and wells of water are produced from the overflow (above). It is like you receive the house and he throws in a car as well. He gives you the job and a company car and condo.

He is able to do exceeding abundantly above all that we ask or "think." Since He is able to go above and beyond what we ask or think, He can do what we haven't even thought about. This deals with **the extreme situations** beyond human comprehension. There are times when I must admit that I don't know what to ask for and I am not sure how to even think about it. Guess what? He can still take care of it. Man's extremities are God's opportunities. In Matthew 19:26, the writer said, "But Jesus beheld them, and said unto them, with men this is impossible; but with God all things are possible." In Luke 1:37, Jesus said, "For with God nothing shall be impossible."

All of the things happen because of **the explosive source** in us. It happens "according to the power that worketh in us" (Ephesians 3:20). This powerful source is the Holy Spirit. The word for *power* is "dunamei" from which we get the word *dynamite*. This explosive power is working in us. It is amazing to see the evidence of the power at work. The Holy Spirit comes into our lives and changes us in ways that even we thought was impossible.

The thought of all of this caused Paul to pause and focus on **the exalted Sovereign** before completing this section of the letter. In Ephesians 3:21, he said, "Unto him be glory in the church by Jesus Christ throughout all ages, world without end. Amen!" This explains why Paul has his "amen moment" before reaching the end of the letter. Paul always ended his letters by saying, "Amen." After writing half of the letter, he says, "Amen!" It is like he is telling us that he can't hold it until the end. I believe he became so excited at this point that he had to drop an extra one (amen) here because he wanted to be his own witness.

Chapter 10

THE EVIDENCE OF THE CONVERSION
EPHESIANS 4:1-6

The Worthy Walk
The Doctrinal Presentation
The Debt Paid
The Designated Position
The Desired Proof
The Daily Practice

The Willing Workers
The Liberated Steppers
The Lord's Servants
The Lip Service
The Lights Shining
The Lowly Spirit

The Lofty Status
The Longsuffering Saint
The Love Shown
The Linked Solidarity

The Wedded Witnesses
The Stamped Relatives
The Spirit Residing
The Scheduled Rapture
The Same Redeemer
The Starting Requirement
The Symbolic Ritual
The Supreme Ruler

THE WORTHY WALK

IN EPHESIANS 1-3, we have dealt with **the doctrinal presentation** in the letter. The doctrinal message focused on

- The eternal plan of God for Christians

- The great blessings of God
- The revealed mystery of God
- The work of God's mercy and love
- The gift of God's grace
- Reconciliation and peace
- The church as the new body of God's people and citizens of the new heaven and earth

As Christians, we should know what we believe. We must possess a solid doctrinal position that we can articulate to others. We should not believe everything we hear from so-called "representatives of God." Paul will address this later on in this chapter.

We could sum up the doctrinal message by addressing **the debt paid** for us to be reconciled to God. Satan had us on lockdown but God sent His Son to set us free. The basic summary of the doctrinal presentation deals with the simple fact that Christ paid the debt so that we could become fellow heirs. The blood shed at Calvary made the difference. We are no longer strangers but fellow heirs through Jesus Christ our Lord. We were reconciled and restored.

All the doctrinal information led to **the designated position** we now have in Christ by grace through faith. We are saved due to our position in Jesus Christ. We are positioned in Christ and His righteousness has been imputed to us. When God looks at us, He sees His Son's blood covering us. We are new creations in Jesus Christ. As a result of being in Christ, the enemy cannot pull us away from the love of God (see Romans 8:35-39). Our position in Christ is secure for eternity. As a matter of fact, our position is so secure that Jesus said, "And I give unto them eternal life; and they shall never perish, neither shall any man pluck them out of my hand" (John 10:28).

Next Paul addresses **the desired proof** of our calling. Paul said, "I therefore, the prisoner of the Lord, beseech you that ye walk worthy of the vocation wherewith ye are called" (Ephesians 4:1). He identifies himself as the prisoner of the Lord just as he did in Ephesians 3:1. Yes, he is in prison in Rome but more importantly, he is a bondservant of the Lord. He pleads with the believers in Ephesus to walk worthy of their vocation.

The worthy walk is seen in **the daily practices** of the believer. The conduct of the believer should reveal his commitment to Christ. We must walk worthy of the vocation daily. It is not just a Sunday practice. When we choose not to walk worthy of the vocation, we dishonor the power that made our salvation possible. In Colossians 1:10, Paul said, "That ye might walk worthy of the Lord unto all pleasing, being fruitful in every good work, and increasing in the knowledge of God."

THE WILLING WORKERS

Yes, Christ has set us free. As a result of being set free, we should be seen as **the liberated steppers** of the Lord. We are walking worthy of the vocation wherewith we are called. The vocation that we have been called to is a reference back to the doctrinal message. He is not talking about vocation as it relates to our careers (doctor, lawyer, teacher, etc.). He is dealing with being called, chosen, and converted from our sinful state. It is not legalistic because the law could not save us. Grace caused it to happen. Neither is it licentiousness. Therefore, we must walk worthy of the honored position to which God has exalted us.

We are **the Lord's servants** and the world should know this. We don't have to wear crosses on chains for people to know we are His disciples. How will they know? They will know by the way we walk. Jesus said, "Wherefore by their fruits ye shall know them" (Matthew 7:20). As we live, people should recognize us as servants of the Lord. People in the neighborhood should know Christians live in the house next door. On your job, they should know that a Christians sits at that desk.

The lip service alone cannot authenticate our commitment. A lot of people claim to know Christ but the walk does not support the claim. The Christian's claim should be accompanied by the worthy walk. Jesus said, "Not every one that saith unto me, Lord, Lord, shall enter into the kingdom of heaven; but he that doeth the will of my Father which is in heaven" (Matthew 7:21). When a believer is walking worthy, he does not have to say a whole lot. His actions speak for him. My grandmother used to sing a song that says, "May the work I've done speak for me. May the life I live speak for me."

The lights shining in this dark world belong to Christians. The vocation wherewith we have been called deals with the fact that God has pulled us out of darkness and placed us in the marvelous light of His glory. As we walk in the light, the glowing should be evident. As we *grow in Christ,* we should *glow for Christ.* As we grow and glow, we can *go* and lead others to the Lord. As the divine spotlight shines on and through us, others will be attracted to the Light of the World.

Paul addresses **the lowly spirit** connected to our walk. We are to walk with all lowliness and meekness (see Ephesians 4:2a). It means to be gentle, tender, and humble. This means to be of low degree and low rank in your actions; not to be high-minded, proud, haughty, or arrogant. A lowly and meek person may have a high position, power, wealth, fame, and much more; but he carries himself in a spirit of lowliness and meekness. We should never become glory seekers (vain glory or empty glory).

Some people just want the attention, the recognition, the position, the flattery, the praise, and the honor. Jesus said, "Take my yoke upon you, and learn of me; for I am meek and lowly in heart: and ye shall find rest unto your souls" (Matthew 11:29). He also said, "And whosoever shall exalt himself shall be abased; and he that shall humble himself shall be exalted" (Matthew 23:12).

This lowly spirit prevents the lofty status from slipping into our lives. When there is a spirit of pride rather than a lowly spirit, it causes people to think they are better than others. They look down on people because they think too highly of themselves. In Philippians, Paul says, "Let nothing be done through strife or vainglory; but in lowliness of mind let each esteem other better than themselves. Look not every man on his own things, but every man also on the things of others" (Philippians 2:3-4).

We are to become the longsuffering saints. The believer is to walk with longsuffering (*makrothumia*). This means that the believer is to walk with patience, bearing and suffering a long time. We are to have perseverance, steadfastness, and endurance. Longsuffering never strikes back. When attacked by others, the natural response is to strike back and retaliate. However, the Christian is given the power to suffer long.

In Colossians 1:11 Paul says, "Strengthened with all might, according to his glorious power, unto all patience and longsuffering with joyfulness." Longsuffering is needed to minister properly. In 2 Timothy, Paul says, "Preach the word; be instant in season, out of season; reprove, rebuke, exhort with all longsuffering and doctrine" (2 Timothy 4:2).

As noted before, the love shown to others is the truest evidence of our conversion. The believer must walk "forbearing one another in love" (see Ephesians 4:2c). *Agape* is unconditional love. The fruit of love goes so far that it loves regardless of feelings (whether a person feels like loving or not); that it loves a person even if the person does not deserve to be loved; that it actually loves the person who is utterly unworthy of being loved.

Throughout the book of Ephesians, Paul addresses the power of the Spirit in the lives of believers. He says, "Endeavoring to keep the unity of the Spirit in the bond of peace" (Ephesians 4:3). The linked solidarity speaks volumes to people in the world. The purpose of walking worthy is to show a body united for Christ. Without unity, our efforts are in vain. Believers are to work at (endeavor) keeping the peace so they can stay bound together in the unity of God's Spirit. There is a spiritual bond of peace produced by the Spirit of God between all believers. As believers, we are to set aside all differences and division; and a spirit of love, peace, and unity should be present.

Stop going around claiming to be saved, sanctified, and filled with the Holy Ghost when there is division and discord between you and others. Solidarity cannot exist when there is prejudice, jealousy, complaining, grumbling, gripes, etc. Paul says, "Now I beseech you, brethren, by the name of our Lord Jesus Christ, that ye speak the same thing, and that there be no divisions among you; but that ye be perfectly joined together in the same mind and in the same judgment" (1 Corinthians 1:10). In 2 Corinthians 13:11, he says, "Finally, brethren, farewell. Be perfect, be of good comfort, be of one mind, live in peace; and the God of love and peace shall be with you."

THE WEDDED WITNESSES

In Ephesians 4:4-6, we see how we are wedded (joined) together as witnesses. As a believer, you are one of many of the stamped relatives in the family of faith. In Ephesians 4:4, Paul said, "There is one body." Every man, woman, boy, and girl accepting Jesus Christ is stamped as a relative of the same body. There are not two bodies or several bodies of believers. Paul said, "So we, being many, are one body in Christ, and every one members one of another" (Romans 12:5).

Yes, there are many different denominations. Yet there is only one body. I love watching the old Westerns like *Bonanza* and *The Big Valley*. The Cartwrights owned cattle on the Ponderosa just like others in Virginia City. The difference between the Cartwrights' cattle and the herds belonging to others was the Ponderosa brand. We have been branded and stamped by our owner, Jesus Christ.

Once again, Paul deals with **the Spirit residing** in the life of all believers. He says, "There is one body, and one Spirit, even as ye are called" (Ephesians 4:4). The same Spirit that dwells within one member of the body dwells in all members of the body. It is God's Spirit that causes a man to be born again. Jesus addressed this fact with Nicodemus in John 3. He said, "Verily, verily, I say unto thee, Except a man be born of water and of the Spirit, he cannot enter into the kingdom of God. That which is born of the flesh is flesh: and that which is born of the Spirit is spirit" (John 3:5-6). Paul says, "For by one Spirit are we all baptized into one body, whether we be Jews or Gentiles, whether we be bond or free; and have been all made to drink into one Spirit" (1 Corinthians 12:13).

Every genuine believer has the same hope of **the scheduled rapture**. It is the hope of the great day of redemption. One day, we will leave, whether dead or alive, to spend eternity with God. This is the "one hope" of our calling (see Ephesians 4:4). Paul addressed this hope in Colossians when he said, "Since we heard of your faith in Christ Jesus, and of the love which ye have to all saints, for the hope which is laid up for you in heaven, whereof ye heard before in the word of the truth of the gospel" (Colossians 1:4-5). In Titus 2:12-13, Paul says, "Teaching us that, denying ungodliness and worldly lusts, we should live soberly, righteously, and godly, in the present world; Looking for that blessed hope, and the glorious appearing of the great God and our Saviour Jesus Christ."

According to Ephesians 4:5, there is only one Lord. Therefore, we have **the same Redeemer**. There is only one Master and King. Every believer has bowed before the same Lord to become His subjects and receive His orders. Paul says, "And there are differences of administrations, but the same Lord" (1 Corinthians 12:5). As noted earlier, all people (not just believers) will acknowledge the one Lord in the future. Paul says, "Wherefore God also hath highly exalted him, and given him a name which is above every name: That at the name of Jesus every knee should bow, of things in heaven, and things in earth, and the things under the earth; And that every tongue should confess that Jesus Christ is Lord, to the glory of God the Father" (Philippians 2:9-11).

There is only "one faith" (see Ephesians 4:5) that leads into God's presence and that is the faith founded by the Lord Jesus Christ. This is **the starting requirement** for all believers. Without this faith, it is impossible to please God. There is no other way to get to the Father except through faith in the Lord Jesus Christ. Paul says, "But what saith it? The word is nigh thee, even in thy mouth, and in thy heart: that is, the word of faith which we preach; That if thou shalt confess with thy mouth the Lord Jesus, and shall believe in thine heart that God hath raised him from the dead, thou shalt be saved" (Romans 10:8-9).

Next Paul deals with **the symbolic ritual** we participate in as believers. He tells us that there is "one baptism" (see Ephesians 4:5). All believers are to publicly show their faith in the Lord by submitting to the ordinance of water baptism. We were publicly initiated by the same ritual. In Romans, Paul says, "Know ye not, that so many of us as were baptized into Jesus Christ were baptized into his death?" (Romans 6:3). In Galatians, he says, "For as many of you as have been baptized into Christ have put on Christ" (Galatians 3:27).

Paul speaks of **the Supreme Ruler** in every believer's life. He says, "One God and Father of all, who is above all, and through all, and in you all" (Ephesians 4:6). Our God is the Creator of all and He is supreme ruler over all. As the supreme ruler, He is above all. He created everything, which means He is through all. Since we were created in God's image, there is a likeness of Him designed to flow through all of us. Now that He lives in the life of every believer, we can function according to our original design. This verse supports our monotheistic belief in one God. The polytheistic belief in many gods must be rejected by believers.

There is none greater than Him. From the beginning of Jesus' earthly ministry until the end, He focused on God our Father. When the disciples asked Jesus to teach them how to pray, He told them to say, "Our Father which art in heaven." His earthly ministry was not about Himself. It was a ministry designed to take care of His Father's business (see Luke 2:49). Before ascending back to His Father, He told the disciples to go back to Jerusalem to wait on the promise of the Father (see Acts 1:4-8).

BELIEVERS BLESSING THE BODY
EPHESIANS 4:7-15

The Victorious Warrior
The Gifted Christians
The Grace Connected
The Great Cost
The Gathered Captives
The Grave Conquered
The Goods Collected
The Glorious Coronation
The Glowing Church

The Valuable Word
The Same Source
The Starting Stage
The Sent Servants
The Special Spokesman

The Scriptural Support
The Sought Sinners
The Selected Shepherds
The Studious Sage

The Veterans Working
The Explained Scripture
The Educated Sheep
The Equipping Stage
The Evolving Steps
The Enlightening Spirit
The Exposed Seducers
The Engaged Servants
The Edified Saints

PAUL CONCLUDED THE last section by focusing on unity (see Ephesians 4:3-6). He said, "Endeavoring to keep the unity of the Spirit in the bond of peace. There is one body, and one

Spirit, even as ye are called in one hope of your calling; One Lord, one faith, one baptism, One God and Father of all."

THE VICTORIOUS WARRIOR

In this section of the epistle, Paul deals with **the gifted Christians** comprising the body. Paul said, "But unto every one of us is given grace according to the measure of the gift of Christ" (Ephesians 4:7). Every believer is gifted. There are no ungifted Christians. None of us was left out. A spiritual gift is the supernatural ability to minister. Paul moves from the unity connected to the whole and addresses the diversity of believers. There are differences between believers when it comes to the special assignments given by God.

Look at **the grace connected** to the gifts received. Jesus gives us the grace to use our gift. The use of the term is different in this context. Normally, we talk about grace as the "unmerited favor" of God. Although this is still true regarding the gifts given to believer, the term in this context means the strength, wisdom, courage, motivation, love, concern, care, and power—all the favor and blessings of Christ.

In Ephesians 4:8, Paul had in mind a picture of a victorious king who has overthrown his foes. Note **the great cost** Christ paid to gain the right to gift believers. He had to die and descend into the lower parts of the earth. Jesus literally had to die and go to hell in order to get us to heaven. Jesus triumphed in battle over sin and Satan. He carried the war into the enemy's domain, Hades.

The primary mission of the king had to do with **the gathered captives.** Paul says, "he led captivity captive" (Ephesians 4:8). Let's go back to the illustration of the king going into the enemy's domain. Yes, He led forth from the lower regions a multitude of captives ("he led captivity captive"). This meant that He goes in and frees the hostages held by the enemy. Although Jesus was physically dead until the third day, He was still spiritually alive. Before Calvary, the godly did not head to heaven.

A good example of this point can be found in the story of the beggar and rich man in Luke 16:19-25. Jesus said, "And it came to pass, that the beggar died, and was carried by the angels into Abraham's bosom: the rich man also died, and was buried; And in hell he lifted up his eyes" (Luke 16:22-23). Did you pay attention to where the beggar went after he died? He was carried by the angels into Abraham's bosom, not heaven. The rich man died and went to hell. Abraham's bosom represents paradise and not heaven.

While physically dead, Jesus goes to hell and preaches to the dead. In 1 Peter 3:18-19, Peter said, "For Christ also hath once suffered for sins, the just for the unjust, that he might bring us to God, being put to death in the flesh, but quickened by the Spirit: by which also he went and preached unto the spirits in prison." He gathered the prisoners of war from the enemy.

Paul says, "Wherefore he saith, when he ascended up on high" (Ephesians 4:8). Here, we see **the grave conquered** by the King. Let's continue with the illustration Paul had in mind. The King is now seen ascending into the mountain and entering triumphantly into the city. No one knew the outcome when He descended into the lower parts but now they can see with the ascension, the victorious King. Yes, it was Easter when His followers discovered Jesus had gained the victory over the grave.

When dealing with Easter, we often describe Jesus as the One who conquered death and the grave when He arose. According to Matthew, the grave was conquered for the dead saints as well. Matthew said, "And the graves were opened; and many bodies of the saints which slept arose, And came out of the graves after his resurrection, and went into the holy city, and appeared unto many" (Matthew 27:52-53). We usually think of Jesus only being victorious over death and the grave. When the Lord arose in triumph, He brought the souls of the blessed dead with Him. Many of them were united with their bodies and shared in His resurrection.

Let's go back to the illustration again. As the king triumphantly enters the city, he is laden with the spoils of war and bestows lavish gifts on his cheering people. He returns to the city with **the goods collected**. Paul says that He "gave gifts unto men" (Ephesians 4:8). Jesus was resurrected with all power in His hands. In Matthew 28:18, Matthew says, "And Jesus came and spake unto them, saying, All power is given unto me in heaven and in earth." In other words, He didn't return empty-handed.

Finally, you see **the glorious coronation** following the war. The last point of the illustration shows the King returning to the throne and taking His rightful place. Jesus Christ is seated at the right hand of God the Father, and He rules and reigns over all. Paul said, "He that descended is the same also that ascended up far above all heavens, that he might fill all things" (Ephesians 4:10). The writer of Hebrews says, "Who being the brightness of his glory, and the express image of his person, and upholding all things by the word of his power, when he had by himself purged our sins, sat down on the right hand of the Majesty on high" (Hebrews 1:3).

He fills all things. The whole earth is full of His presence. How? We have **the glowing church** filled with gifted people. Yes, the shining lights mentioned earlier cause the whole earth to be full of His presence. Jesus said, "Ye are the light of the world. A city that is set on a hill cannot be hid . . . Let your light so shine before men, that they may see your good works, and glorify your Father which is in heaven" (Matthew 5:14, 16).

THE VALUABLE WORD

Paul says, "And He gave some, apostles; and some, prophets; and some, evangelists; and some, pastors and teachers" (Ephesians 4:11). He gave. **The same source** is responsible for the giftedness of the body, the church of Jesus Christ. If He is not the giver of the supernatural abilities, you can add one word before each position listed in Ephesians 4:11 (false apostle, false prophet, false evangelist, etc.). The common denominator for each of the gifts in Ephesians 4:11 is the Word of God. Therefore, we are dealing with gifts bestowed on the church or body (universal) rather than the individuals in the body (1 Corinthians 12). These gifts are designed to deal with the formation, foundation, flow, and function of the church universal.

Paul begins this section focusing on **the starting stage** of the church. When the church was birthed, there was not a book in print called the Bible. The completion of the New Testament canon of Scripture did not come until the end of the first century. Yet the early saints needed a word from the Lord. They needed the apostles and prophets during the formative years of the church. We have discussed this already. In Ephesians 2:20, Paul said, "And are built upon the foundation of the apostles and prophets, Jesus Christ himself being the chief corner stone."

They had the apostles, also known as **the sent servants** of God. The word *apostle* (*apostolos*) means to send out. An apostle is a representative or ambassador who is sent to represent the leader or ruler. You had the primary and secondary apostles listed in the Bible. The primary apostles refer to the twelve and to Paul. The apostles were chosen directly by the Lord. The apostle had been an eyewitness of the resurrected Lord. The word *apostle* refers to others preaching the gospel in the Bible (Barnabas, Titus, Silas, etc.).

Paul deals with **the special spokesmen**. The gift of the prophet dealt with the ones speaking under the inspiration of God's Spirit that included both prediction and proclamation. The New Testament prophets were not like the Old Testament prophets who predicted or prophesied doom and disaster. In 1 Corinthians 14:3, Paul said, "But he that prophesieth speaketh unto men to edification, and exhortation, and comfort."

Let me comment on **the Scriptural support** for all of the ones listed in Ephesians 4:11. In our day and time, there are a lot of people claiming to be apostles and prophets. They use the terms in their titles. In all honesty, I really struggle with this misinterpretation of this text. Yet I don't spend a lot of time speaking against the use of the titles. My greatest concern is not with the titles but the lack of truth often flowing from the lips of those with the titles. If the Scripture does not line up with what they are saying, they are not connected to Jesus Christ and you need to beware. If they are speaking anything other than the Word of God, you need to ignore them.

Now look at the gift of an evangelist. **The sought sinner** is the primary focus of the evangelist. This is the gift of carrying the gospel all over the world. This gift specializes in proclaiming the gospel to the lost souls of the world. One of the original deacons had this gift. In Acts 21:8, Luke said, "And the next day we that were of Paul's company departed, and came unto Caesarea: and we entered into the house of Philip the evangelist, which was one of the seven; and abode with him." The one with this gift has the supernatural ability to draw people to Christ with the Word of God.

Next we have the gift of a pastor (*poimenas*). The word means shepherd. **The selected shepherd** is really an under-shepherd to the Chief Shepherd, Christ Jesus our Lord. The under-shepherd should seek to imitate the Chief Shepherd. What does this mean?

- The shepherd knows the sheep. "I am the good shepherd, and know my sheep, and am known of mine" (John 10:14).
- The shepherd feeds the flock. (Do you love me Peter? Feed my sheep.)
- The shepherd guides the sheep to the pasture and away from the rough places. "The Lord is my shepherd; I shall not want. He maketh me to lie down in green pastures: he leadeth me beside the still waters. He restoreth my soul: he leadeth me in the paths of righteousness for his name's sake" (Psalm 23:1-3).

- The shepherd protects and secures the sheep. "Yea, though I walk through the valley of the shadow of death, I will fear no evil: for thou art with me; thy rod and thy staff they comfort me" (Psalm 23:4). By the way, He prepares a table in the presence of their enemies in Psalm 23:5. As I preach, I am preparing a table for the sheep and I don't care if the enemy is around.
- The shepherd seeks the lost sheep. In Luke 15, the shepherd leaves the ninety-nine to go and find the one lost.
- The shepherd strives to keep the sheep separate from the goats.

The spiritual gift of teaching is the gift of understanding and communicating the Word of God. Like most theologians, I believe this gift is linked to the pastor. The pastor must be **the studious sage.** I believe Paul is dealing with the giftedness of the pastor/teacher. Paul said, "Study to shew thyself approved unto God, a workman that needeth not to be ashamed, rightly dividing the word of truth" (2 Timothy 2:15). The function of the teacher is to instruct believers in the truth of God and His Word. In 2 Timothy 3:16, Paul said, "All scripture is given by inspiration of God, and is profitable for doctrine, for reproof, for correction, and for instruction in righteousness." Every pastor should have the gift of teaching, but every gifted teacher is not a pastor.

THE VETERANS WORKING

Paul says, "For the perfecting of the saints, for the work of the ministry, for the edifying of the body of Christ" (Ephesians 4:12). With all of the titles mentioned, the goal is to make the message plain enough for the hearer to understand. **The explained Scripture** will cause the church to become all that God desires. For example, the primary function of the pastor-teacher is to deliver expository sermons to the sheep. The pastor-teacher must explain the Scriptures in such a way that people understand the message so they can apply it to their lives.

The educated sheep should always be the primary mission of the pastor-teacher in the church. In Matthew 28:20, Jesus said, "Teaching them to observe all things whatsoever I have commanded you: and, lo, I am with you always, even unto the end of the world. Amen." We are all called to be students of the Word. It is hard to educate the student or sheep if they never avail themselves of the teaching. The students must avail themselves to be taught the truth. You can't come to church three or four times a year and learn a lot. It is like the college student who never goes to class. You can't learn that way.

After receiving Christ and learning more about Him, **the equipping stage** should follow. We must become equipped to serve Him faithfully. Every believer should strive to grow in Christ. The Word of God perfects or matures us. Knowledge equips us. Ignorance stunts our growth. We cannot serve as God intended if we are not receiving and applying His Word to our lives. Yes, we all start off as babes in Christ but we are not to stay there. "When I was a child, I spoke as a child, I understood as a child, I thought as a child: but when I became a man I put away childish things" (1 Corinthians 13:11).

Spiritual growth is all about **the evolving steps**. The ultimate goal is to "grow up" as believers. The subject of spiritual growth is so important that Paul deals with it again in the next two verses. In Ephesians 4:13, he says, "Till we all come in the unity of the faith, and of the knowledge of the Son of God, unto a perfect man, unto the measure of the stature of the fulness of Christ." As long as we are on this earth, we are to keep learning until we "come in" the unity of the faith. The pastor-teacher is to lead people into harmony. The pastor-teacher is to shepherd people out of cliques and divisiveness.

This evolving step is also seen in Ephesians 4:15 when Paul says, "But speaking the truth in love, may grow up into him in all things, which is the head, even Christ." The goal is to move gradually through the spiritual stages of development. Peter said, "Wherefore laying aside all malice, and all guile, and hypocrisies, and envies, and all evil speaking, As newborn babes, desire the sincere milk of the word, that ye may grow thereby" (1 Peter 2:1-2). "But strong meat belongs to them that are of full age, even those who by reason of use have their senses exercised to discern both good and evil" (Hebrews 5:14).

The pastor-teacher cannot be effective without **the enlightening Spirit** being involved. It does not matter how gifted the pastor-teacher may be; the student must ultimately be enlightened by the Spirit of God. Jesus said, "Howbeit when he, the Spirit of truth, is come, he will guide you into all truth" (John 16:13). He will cause the light to come on so that we grasp the Word of God.

Paul said, "That we henceforth be no more children, tossed to and fro, and carried about with every wind of doctrine, by the sleight of men, and cunning craftiness, whereby they lie in wait to deceive" (Ephesians 4:14). Let me comment on **the exposed seducers** when a believer has become educated, equipped, and enlightened. Yes, there are imposters operating in all of the categories mentioned in Ephesians 4:11. In Matthew 7:15, Jesus said, "Beware of false prophets, which come to you in sheep's clothing, but inwardly they are ravening wolves." In Matthew 15:9, Jesus said, "But in vain they do worship me, teaching for doctrines the commandments of men."

Eventually, the educated sheep should become **the engaged servants** of God. Let's go back to Ephesians 4:12. The pastor-teacher must equip the saints for *the work of the ministry*. Every believer should be actively engaged in ministry. In Matthew 9:37-38, Jesus said, "The harvest truly is plenteous, but the laborers are few; Pray ye therefore the Lord of the harvest, that he will send forth laborers into his harvest." God is looking for equipped laborers to take care of the harvest.

Paul concludes this section by addressing **the edified saints**. The pastor-teacher must equip the saints for the work of the ministry and for the edifying of the body of Christ (see Ephesians 4:12). The word *edify* means "to build up." The work of ministry includes encouraging and edifying other believers. We have been called and chosen to support one another.

Chapter 12

GIFTEDNESS WITHOUT GODLINESS
EPHESIANS 4:16-24

The Gifted Body
The Weak Congregation
The Whole Church
The Watching Crew
The Workload Covered
The Worker's Commitment
The Workforce's Charity
The Walk Considered

The Gentile's Behavior
The Devilish Concentration
The Darkened Comprehension
The Detached Children
The Defiant Conduct

The Defunct Conscience
The Debauchery Celebrated
The Defiled Condition
The Deep Craving

The Godly Believer
The Role Model
The Revealed Message
The Removable Mess
The Renewed Mind
The Regenerated Man
The Remarkable Metamorphosis
The Righteousness Manifested
The Reachable Mark

GIFTEDNESS WITHOUT GODLINESS is like putting cologne or perfume on a stinking body. The cologne does not cover or conceal the stench; it creates a different odor that is awful. The two don't mix. Ephesians 4:16 is the concluding verse about the gifts. Let's look at the summary about the gifts in this verse.

THE GIFTED BODY

God has given every gift needed for the church to be strong and viable. **The weak congregation** is the one in which the gifts are not used or they are used improperly. Paul said, "From whom the whole body fitly joined together and compacted by that which every joint supplieth, according to the effectual working in the measure of every part, maketh increase of the body unto the edifying of itself in love" (Ephesians 4:16). Every *joint or every believer* supplies something to the body of Christ (the church). Therefore, a weak congregation can exist when the believers are not operating in their giftedness.

Paul is dealing with **the whole church** in this passage. He says, "From whom the whole body fitly joined together" (Ephesians 4:16). The whole church is fitly joined together like the links in a chain. When there is a weak link in the chain, it is difficult to operate at the level God intended.

Let's deal with **the watching crew** in the church. God did not save any of us so that we could sit idly by and do nothing. It is hard to accomplish all that God intended with the crew watching from the sidelines in our churches. It is sad that there are so many Christians sitting back, watching and expecting others to do all of the work. You repeatedly ask them to do their part and there is no change. Paul said, "From whom the whole body fitly joined together and compacted by that which every joint supplieth" (Ephesians 4:16). My work is impacted by your work. The work is all connected.

He said, "according to the effectual working in the measure of every part" (see Ephesians 4:16b). **The workload covered** by a few members is not as impactful as the workload covered by all members. The hand cannot do what the foot does but both are needed to carry out the assignment. Every joint is to work "in the measure of every part." The measure is important here. The finger cannot do what the whole hand can do but the hand could not do much without the help of each finger. You may be a finger instead of a hand, but you are just as valuable.

We had a brother here years ago who would go into the classroom every Sunday morning and write on the board historical facts about the person or place in the Sunday school lesson. This person would never stand before the class and teach a lesson because he didn't have the gift of teaching. He possessed the gifts of helps and knowledge. Yet he was just as valuable as the teacher.

The worker's commitment draws others into the fold. He said, "maketh increase of the body. . . . " When people witness this commitment of the exercised gifts, it draws others to become a part of the body.

As gifted as we may be, **the workforce's charity** is the most important part of the process. He concludes Ephesians 4:16 by saying, "unto the edifying of itself in love." In another section written by Paul concerning the abuse of the gifts of the Spirit, he concludes the chapter in 1 Corinthians 13 by saying, "Now, abideth faith, hope, charity; but the greatest of these is charity."

The walk connected to the gifted person makes a difference. The walk or lifestyle will determine the effectiveness of your gift. Paul says, "This I say therefore, and testify in the Lord, that ye henceforth walk not as other Gentiles walk" (Ephesians 4:17). Let's not forget that Paul is writing to Gentiles. The church at Ephesus was a Gentile church. He instructs and exhorts them to no longer walk as Gentiles walk. The point is real simple here. Believers are not to walk as other men walk.

THE GENTILE'S BEHAVIOR

Gentiles walk in "the vanity of their mind" (Ephesians 4:17b). This deals with **the devilish concentration** of the Gentile before

Christ. The word *vain* means devoid, empty, and futile. The word *mind* (*nous*) means thoughts and concentration. The Gentile's mind is void and empty of God and His truth. God is not in their thoughts. God has been pushed out of their minds. Their concentration focuses on worldly pleasures, possessions, power, and position. In Genesis, the writer says, "And God saw that the wickedness of man was great in the earth, and that every imagination of the thoughts of his heart was only evil continually" (Genesis 6:5). In Proverbs 15, the writer says, "The thoughts of the wicked are an abomination to the Lord" (Proverbs 15:26).

The devilish concentration is always accompanied by **the darkened comprehension**. Paul said that their understanding was darkened (see Ephesians 4:18a). To understand means to grasp, comprehend, perceive. To be darkened means to be blinded and unable to see. In Proverbs, the writer says, "The way of the wicked is as darkness: they know not at what they stumble" (Proverbs 4:19).

The unbeliever does not grasp or comprehend God because he is blind and unable to see God. In 2 Corinthians 4:4, Paul says, "In whom the god of this world hath blinded the minds of them which believe not, lest the light of the glorious gospel of Christ, who is the image of God, should shine unto them." In 2 Timothy 3:7, he says, "Ever learning, and never able to come to the knowledge of the truth."

The reason for the devilish concentration and darkened comprehension is due to them "being alienated from the life of God through the ignorance that is in them, because of the blindness of their heart" (Ephesians 4:18b). **The detached children** do not have a heart for God. As unbelievers, they are spiritually detached, dead, and doomed to eternal death. They do not possess the life source and support mentioned earlier.

The "blindness of their heart" leads to **the defiant conduct**. It would be wrong to expect ungodly people to behave godly if their hearts have been blinded to the truth. The behavioral system operates according to the belief system in place.

Next Paul deals with **the defunct conscience** of the Gentile. Paul says, "Who being past feeling have given themselves over unto lasciviousness, to work all uncleanness with greediness" (Ephesians 4:19). When a person is "past feeling," the active conscience no longer exists. To be past feeling means to become callous and hardened. The more a person walks in sin, the more callous his conscience becomes to righteousness. Sin becomes more and more acceptable. The person's conscience no longer bothers him. In 1 Timothy, Paul says, "Speaking lies in hypocrisy: having their conscience seared with a hot iron" (1 Timothy 4:2).

To make matters worse, you see **the debauchery celebrated** by the person who has his conscience seared. They have given themselves over to lasciviousness according to Ephesians 4:19. Lasciviousness deals with all forms of sensual living. The term means indecency and shamelessness. Therefore, it is shameless indecency. It is a person who sins so much that he no longer cares what people say or think. When a person misbehaves, he usually tries to hide his wrong but a lascivious person does not care who knows about it.

Next he mentions **the defiled condition** of the Gentile when he uses the phrase "to work all uncleanness" in Ephesians 4:19. The word *uncleanness* means to be dirty, defiled, contaminated, and filthy. As a kid, I lived on a farm in Camden, Arkansas. My father raised pigs on the farm. One day, my brother and I decided to take one of the pigs covered in mud and spray it down with the water hose. After cleaning up the pig, we smiled at our accomplishment. As we called our sister out to see the clean pig, it escaped our grasp. When my sister came out, she saw a muddy pig because it found the nearest mud puddle to waddle into. In a real sense, we were just like that pig before Christ. The law could not clean us up because of our nature "to work all uncleanness."

The word *greediness* in Ephesians 4:19 deals with the deep craving for more. It means to covet and crave what you don't have and to do what is necessary to get it. The problem is that receiving it does not satisfy the craving. You keep wanting more and more. It is like having an addiction to a drug in which you do whatever it takes to support your habit. There is a continuous hunger for sinful things. In Romans 3, Paul describes them by saying, "Their feet are swift to shed blood: Destruction and misery are in their ways: And the way of peace have they not known: There is no fear of God before their eyes" (Romans 3:15-18).

THE GODLY BELIEVER

The role model for the godly believer is Jesus Christ. Paul says, "If so be that ye have heard him, and have been taught by him, as the truth is in Jesus" (Ephesians 4:21). The believer is to walk in Christ. He is not to walk as men walk. The reason is clearly stated: Believers did not learn such a sinful life from Christ.

In Ephesians 4:21, Paul is dealing with the revealed message connected to the life of Christ. They had not literally heard Him or been taught by Him. The message about His life and death had been revealed to them. The message revealed that Christ did not live a sinful life. He has not taught us to live a sinful life as other men live. If a man has heard Christ and been taught by Christ, then he has heard and been taught the truth. Note that the Teacher is Christ Himself, not the minister or the Sunday school teacher. By the Holy Spirit, Christ uses the voices of the pastors, teachers, and evangelists to teach people how they are to live, but Jesus should always serve as the role model.

In Ephesians 4:22, he says, "That ye put off concerning the former conversation of the old man." This verse addresses the removable mess that we can get rid of after surrendering our lives to Christ. The Greek word *anastrophe* is used thirteen times in the New Testament and is always translated *conversation* in the King

James text. The true meaning in today's English is "manner of life." Paul was saying that the true believer is to put off or remove his former manner of life. In a way, each believer has received a new suit of clothes and so we can take off our old sin-stained garments. We are not to try to wear the new clothes over the old. He reminds us that the old man was corrupt and contaminated. He says, "That ye put off concerning the former conversation the old man, which is corrupt according to the deceitful lusts" (Ephesians 4:22). Paul is describing the old nature with its deceitful desires that produced corruption. He says, "Put it off!"

He says, "And be renewed in the spirit of your mind" (Ephesians 4:23). **The renewed mind** is the key to living a holy life. Without God, we cannot think properly about matters of faith and morals. Satan always attacks the mind and this is why we need the helmet of salvation.

In Ephesians 4:24a, he says, "And that ye put on the new man." The new man is **the regenerated man.** He has been born again. The new nature is the nature of Christ. When we were born in this world, we took on the nature of the first Adam. We were born sinners. When we became born again, we took on the nature of the second Adam. In Romans 5:19, Paul says, "For as by one man's disobedience many were made sinners, so by the obedience of one shall many be made righteous."

When a person has been regenerated, **the remarkable metamorphosis** that takes place on the inside is unexplainable. It is amazing to see how God changes the heart of man. Before Christ, the heart is dark and dirty (see Ephesians 4:18). After regeneration, God creates a clean heart in the life of the believer. David understood that no one could do this but God. He said, "Create in me a clean heart, O God; and renew a right spirit within me" (Psalm 51:10). The blood of Christ is the cleansing agent used to create new hearts. The songwriter said, "What can wash away my sins? What can make me whole again?" He goes on to say, "Nothing but the blood of Jesus."

As a result of the remarkable metamorphosis on the inside, **the righteous manifestation** becomes visible on the outside. He says, "which after God is created in righteousness and true holiness" (Ephesians 4:24b). The visible evidence of the inward change is also remarkable. The new birth leads to righteous and holy behavior. The lifestyle changes as a result of the clean heart. I heard my grandfather say, "I looked at my hands and my hands look new. I looked at my feet and they did too." Well, I didn't see new hands and new feet after I was converted. However, my hands stopped doing a lot of the things I used to do and my feet stopped taking me to places I used to go.

True holiness becomes **the reachable mark** for all believers. Without God, holy living is unrealistic and unreachable. After conversion, it becomes reachable when we allow the Spirit of God to take over our lives. In other words, before Christ, I sinned because I was a sinner. Now I don't have to engage in sin because of the power residing in me. I am holy because of my position in Christ. I can also practice holiness because of the power of Christ. Paul said, "Brethren, I count not myself to have apprehended: but this one thing I do, forgetting those things which are behind, and reaching forth unto those things which are before, I press toward the mark for the prize of the high calling of God in Christ Jesus" (Philippians 3:13-14).

Chapter 13

THE WORST DRESSED CATEGORY
EPHESIANS 4:25-29

The Dead Trespasser
The Dignified Temples
The Devised Temptations
The Deceptive Tongue
The Declared Truth
The Deviation Technique
The Disciples Targeted
The Designed Temperament
The Dangerous Temper
The Devil's Tools

The Delayed Time
The Divine Throne
The Delivered Thief
The Dutiful Toiler
The Disciple's Task
The Dependable Trustee
The Distasteful Talk
The Deplorable Thoughts
The Diabolical Terms
The Destroyed Teammate

WHEN THE ACADEMY Awards are presented, there is a lot of hoopla concerning the attire worn by the Hollywood stars. There is the "Best Dressed" category in which the reporters, along with fashion design critics, comment on the stunning attire. They often select celebrities for the "Worst Dressed" category.

In the last chapter, we concluded with the following points from Ephesians 4:24: "And that ye put on the new man, which after God is created in righteousness and true holiness."

We learned early in this book that we were dead in trespasses and sins before Christ. As a result of receiving Christ in your life, you have become **the dead trespasser**. The trespasser should have died when the new life began. In Romans 6:6-7, Paul says, "Knowing this, that our old man is crucified with him, that the body of sin might be destroyed, that henceforth we should not serve sin. For he that is dead is freed from sin." In the past we served sin because we were born sinners. It was our nature (the old man) that caused us to live in sin. After the new birth, the old man was crucified.

Let's not forget that Paul is writing to the church and not to people in the world. In other writings, he has described each of us as **the dignified temples** bought with a price. As temples of God, we are now people of honor or esteem. In 2 Corinthians 6:16, Paul says, "And what agreement hath the temple of God with idols? For ye are the temple of the living God; as God hath said, I will dwell in them, and walk in them: and I will be their God, and they shall be my people." His light shines through us as we live and walk.

As believers, we are no longer gripped by Satan, but don't let your guard down. It is true that you have been brought out of darkness and placed in the marvelous light. However, Satan will come after you with **the devised temptations** to match what you did while you were living in darkness. As a matter of fact, he takes his assaults to another level because of your commitment to Christ.

How can this happen when the old man has been crucified? The answer is simple. There is a constant battle taking place between the Spirit and the flesh in you. We only walk in victory when we walk after the Spirit. In Romans 8:1, Paul says, "There is therefore now no condemnation to them which are in Christ Jesus, who walk not after the flesh, but after the Spirit." Satan realizes that the flesh was not removed when you turned your life over to Christ. Therefore, he devises temptations to try and lure us from walking after the Spirit.

In Ephesians 4:25, Paul says, "Wherefore putting away lying, speak every man truth with his neighbour: for we are members one of another." **The deceptive tongue** must be put away. Paul said that the believer is to strip away the garment of lying. The garment of lying (*pseudo*) means that which is false. It is untruthfulness, deception, and exaggeration. A liar hides the truth. The deceptive tongue is connected to the old nature when Satan controlled us. Jesus said, "Ye are of your father the devil and the lusts of your father ye will do. He was a murderer from the beginning, and abode not in the truth, because there is no truth in him. When he speaketh a lie, he speaketh of his own: for he is a liar, and the father of it" (John 8:44).

Paul now deals with **the declared truth**. He says, "Speak every man truth with his neighbor: for we are members one of another" (Ephesians 4:25). When speaking about the tongue, James says, "But the tongue can no man tame; it is an unruly evil, full of deadly poison" (James 3:8). The lying tongue is poisonous and destructive. Since the tongue cannot be tamed, it must be transformed. It is the transformed tongue that tells the truth.

Let me comment on **the deviation technique** that is just as damaging as the lies people tell. The word *deviate* means "not direct" or "not straightforward." This is the liar that camouflages the truth. There are people who sprinkle a little truth in their comments to make you think they are telling it all. The declared truth must be the whole truth and nothing but the truth. We can be guilty of only telling truthful parts. A truthful part is still equivalent to a whole lie. By the way, the word *deviate* comes from the same family as the words *devious* and *devilish*.

Paul also deals with **the disturbing target** of some of the deception. He says, "For we are members one of another" (Ephesians 4:25). Paul is instructing the church to put away lying and to start speaking truth. Paul reminds us that we are members of one body. Paul is instructing us to stop lying to all people. Yet he places emphasis on how disturbing it is to see this happening in the church among believers. We should never be surprised when people in the world deceive us because it is part of their nature. When other members of the family use deceptive words and ways, it should shock us.

In Ephesians 4:26-27, Paul says, "Be ye angry, and sin not: let not the sun go down upon your wrath: Neither give place to the devil." There are several points to make about these verses. Let's deal with **the designed temperament**. It is normal to become angry because this is an emotion connected to our designed temperament. There is "righteous anger" or justifiable anger. The believer must be angry with those who sin and do wrong and who are unjust and selfish in their behavior to a certain degree that I will explain in a moment. God expects righteous anger.

Let's talk about **the dangerous temper**. There is also wrong or unjustified anger. Becoming angry is not a sin but Paul is addressing the dangerous temper that some people possess. We need to know how to properly manage anger. This is the anger that harbors malice; it will not forget; it lingers; it broods; it seeks revenge; it hopes for bad things to happen to others. In Romans, Paul says, "If it be possible, as much as lieth in you, live peaceably with all men" (Romans 12:18).

This type of anger is **the devil's tool** to disrupt divine harmony. In Ephesians 4:27, Paul said, "Neither give place to the devil." One of the devil's tactics or tools is to convince us to use retaliatory responses against people who have upset us. The psalmist says, "Cease from anger, and forsake wrath: fret not thyself in any wise to do evil" (Psalm 37:8). James says, "Wherefore, my beloved brethren, let every man be swift to hear, slow to speak, slow to wrath" (James 1:19). The devil's tools are always designed to cause us to do devilish things.

Another point to make about this verse deals with **the delayed time** in which we address issues. Now let's go back to "not letting the sun go down on your wrath." This means that you should try to discuss the topic as soon as possible. In Ecclesiastes 7:9, the writer says, "Be not hasty in thy spirit to be angry: for anger resteth in the bosom of fools" (Ecclesiastes 7:9). Why should we discuss the dividing issue as soon as possible and not let the sun go down without resolving the matter? The devil will try to cause the anger to degenerate to sin. He desires wrath to flow from you against your offender. If you give the devil time, he will try to convince you to respond in an ungodly manner. The writer of Proverbs says, "He that is slow to anger is better than the mighty; and he that ruleth his spirit than he that taketh a city" (Proverbs 16:32).

The last point to make about Ephesians 4:27-28 deals with approaching **the divine throne** to release all bitterness. In some cases, it is not a matter of going to the person. The person you are angry with may be dead and gone. Yet you still find yourself angry and bitter over the offense committed against you. It is important for you to take the necessary steps to deal with the anger because past pain can have an effect on the present condition. You need to go directly to the throne of God in order to move beyond it. You may not be able to meet with the person who made you angry. However, you can always go to the Lord to help you deal with your anger.

In Ephesians 4:28, Paul says, "Let him that stole steal no more: but rather let him labor, working with his hands the thing which is good, that he may have to give to him that needeth." As a believer, you are now **the delivered thief**. Paul basically says, "If you were a thief before Christ, you should stop stealing since you are saved." The word *steal* (*klepto*) means to cheat, to take wrongfully from another person. Peter says, "But let none of you suffer as a murderer, or as a thief" (1 Peter 4:15).

Paul deals with **the dutiful toiler** when he says, "Let him that stole steal no more: but rather let him labor, *working with his hands the thing which is good*" (Ephesians 4:28, emphasis added). In essence, Paul is saying that the person should get a job to earn a living. Go to work! Before concluding the letter to the Ephesians, Paul will discuss the believer's work ethic (see Ephesians 6:5-9).

After working to earn a wage, **the disciple's task** is to be a blessing to those who are less fortunate. We are to give to the needy. The point is not just about giving to the needy here. The task reveals that you have changed from a taker to a giver. It also reveals that your labor has not only caused you to receive enough to take care of your personal needs; you have received extra to be a blessing to others.

A person is quick to quote Philippians 4:19 when they want God to provide for them. "But my God shall supply all your need according to his riches in glory by Christ Jesus." This verse is for **the dependable trustee** of God. God should be able to trust and depend on us when He blesses us. Philippians 4 focuses on the saints in Philippi sending a love offering to Paul while he was imprisoned in Rome. As a result of their willingness to bless others, Paul informed them that God would supply all of their needs. It really boils down to whether or not God can trust you with the blessings.

In Ephesians 4:29, Paul says, "Let no corrupt communication proceed out of your mouth, but that which is good to the use of edifying, that it may minister grace unto the hearers." Believers must rid themselves of **the distasteful talk** designed to destroy lives. The word *corrupt* (*sapros*) means rotten, foul, and polluting. Corrupt talk would include cursing and unholy talk. In Romans 3:13-14, Paul says, "Their throat is an open sepulcher; with their tongues they have used deceit; the poison of asps is under their lips; Whose mouth is full of cursing and bitterness." An open grave with a decomposing body is foul.

Now that you are saved, all corrupt communication should leave a bad taste in your mouth. James says, "And the tongue is a fire, a world of iniquity: so is the tongue among our members, that it defileth the whole body, and setteth on fire the course of nature; and it is set on fire of hell" (James 3:6). In the psalmist's prayer, he said, "Set a watch, O Lord, before my mouth; keep the door of my lips" (Psalm 141:3).

The distasteful talk flows from **the deplorable thoughts** in our minds. Before you curse out someone, lie on someone, or speak evil to someone, the thought of the act occurs first. This is why we discussed the renewed mind and the clean heart earlier. Jesus said, "For out of the heart proceed evil thoughts, murders, adulteries, fornication, thefts, false witness, blasphemies" (Matthew 15:19). You must start thinking right in order to start talking and acting right.

We should get rid of **the diabolical terms** that we have stored in our vocabulary. As a believer, all profanity and vulgarity should be removed from your speaking. You should not be guilty of cursing people out. In Colossians, Paul says, "But now ye also put off all these: anger, wrath, malice, blasphemy, filthy communication out of your mouth" (Colossians 3:8).

In conclusion, the deceptive tongue and the distasteful talk can lead to **the destroyed teammate**. Paul says that believers are to speak "that which is good to the use of edifying that it may minister grace unto the hearers" (Ephesians 4:29). The old adage is really not true that says, "Sticks and stones may break my bones but words will never hurt me." Words can do a lot of damage. We are to speak words that edify and minister grace instead of words that damage and destroy. We are to build up one another and not tear down one another. In Proverbs 16:24, the writer says, "Pleasant words are as a honeycomb, sweet to the soul, and health to the bones."

Chapter 14

GRIEVING THE GOD IN YOU
EPHESIANS 4:30-32

The Received Partner
The Convicted Sinner
The Converted Soul
The Changed Status
The Christian Sealed
The Comforter Stationed
The Constant Struggle
The Correct Steps
The Contrary Servant
The Created Sadness
The Crushed Spirit

The Remodeled Premises
The Reliable Source

The Residing Resentment
The Retaliation Rendered
The Recognized Root
The Released Rage
The Ruined Reputation

The Righteousness Practiced
The Caring Family
The Commended Favor
The Compassionate Friend
The Commanded Forgiveness
The Caring Father
The Created Flashbacks
The Covered Faults

WHILE GROWING UP in Arkansas, I used to follow my grandfather to the different churches where he served as pastor. He was one of those circuit pastors that had three different charismatic churches in several small towns in the rural area of Arkansas. During the services, they had what they called a testimonial period in which members of the congregation would come before the church and share a testimony.

They would always say the same thing as their opening statement. They would say, "I thank God that I am saved, sanctified, and filled with the Holy Ghost" before sharing different testimonies. As a kid, I was somewhat confused by the opening statement because I heard some of them saying some words before service started that were not godly. I saw some doing some ungodly things during the week that did not support a life filled with the Holy Ghost. As I grew up, I soon learned that simply saying it did not mean that it was true.

THE RECEIVED PARTNER

You didn't start off as a spiritual person. One day, you became **the convicted sinner.** This is when the Spirit first came on the scene in your life and started pricking your heart. This process started the very moment you reached the age in which you started noticing the difference between right and wrong. The Spirit of God started convicting your conscience as a child when you violated the rules.

At some point following the convicting periods, the Holy Spirit's actions led to **the converted soul** in you. He convinced you that Jesus Christ was needed in your life and one day you surrendered your life to God. The light came on and you confessed with your mouth and believed in your heart the redemptive work of Jesus Christ. At the moment of your conversion, floods of joy filled your soul because the Spirit of God moved in.

Before the Spirit convicted and converted us, we were sinners destined for hell. God came into our lives and our identity and destination changed. The work of the Holy Spirit is responsible for **the changed status** in your life. At the moment of conversion, we became saints. The sinful slate has been cleared for every believer.

We are no longer hell-bound sinners but heaven-bound saints with His Spirit residing in our lives. What is the role of the Holy Spirit in the life of the believer? The primary work of the Holy Spirit is to keep **the Christian sealed** until the day of redemption. Paul says, "And grieve not the Holy Spirit of God, whereby ye are sealed unto the day of redemption" (Ephesians 4:30). I will deal with what it means to grieve the Holy Spirit later in this chapter. The point I want to make now deals with the flow of the verse. It is important to see that grieving does not break the seal. We will remain divinely sealed until the day of redemption. In other words, as a believer, you can expect the Holy Spirit to remain in your life at all times.

Since the Holy Spirit stays with us, this means that we have **the Comforter stationed** in our lives on this earthly journey. In the Gospel of John, Jesus said, "And I will pray the Father, and he shall give you another Comforter, that he may abide with you forever" (John 14:16). The Holy Spirit is able to provide comfort in uncomfortable situations. He doesn't prevent the blows of life from coming; He simply softens the blows once they arrive.

It is true that you have been sealed by the Holy Spirit but you still have to deal with **the constant struggles** between the flesh and the Spirit. When the Spirit of God moved in, the flesh did not move out. Before the Spirit of God entered the life of the believer, the flesh ruled and reigned. Now that the Spirit resides, there is a constant battle taking place. The flesh still has the power to control the life of the believer if we have not allowed the Spirit of God to take charge. In Romans 7:18-19, Paul says, "For I know that in me (that is, in my flesh,) dwelleth no good thing: for to will is present with me; but how to perform that which is good I find not. For the good that I would, I do not: but the evil which I would not, that I do."

The constant struggle does not mean we cannot live in victory. The Holy Spirit will prevail if we allow Him to show us **the correct steps** to receive victory over the flesh. As growing believers,

He is stationed in our lives to help us walk worthy. He is more powerful than any temptation or trap produced by the enemy. We only have to submit to Him as our Guide and Guard.

The Holy Spirit will never force us to obey. When we fail to obey, we lose out. In a sense, **the contrary servant** causes the Spirit of God to work overtime. The Holy Spirit shows us the correct steps to take but we become contrary and do our own thing and end up witnessing consequences that could have been avoided had we been compliant rather than defiant. He tells us to go right and we go left and start complaining when we end up stuck in the mud of life.

Paul deals with **the created sadness** sin causes for the Holy Spirit. Paul says, "And grieve not the Holy Spirit of God, whereby ye are sealed unto the day of redemption" (Ephesians 4:30). The word *grieve* basically means "to become sad." As noted earlier, the Holy Spirit is stationed in the believer's life at all times. Therefore, when we go left when He told us to go right, we end up taking Him in that same sinful direction because He is in us. He is called the *Holy* Spirit, which means He is holy. When we participate in unholy activities, He becomes grieved. He is saddened by the sinful steps taken when we should have been submissive to His instructions.

Paul is also dealing with **the crushed Spirit** in this verse. Every believer should seek to be filled with the Spirit. This is God's desire for us. There is a difference between the indwelling and the infilling of the Spirit. The moment you accept Jesus Christ, the Holy Spirit indwells the life of the believer. As you grow in the faith and surrender your life to Him, the infilling occurs. When we are filled with the Holy Spirit, we have basically allowed Him to take complete control. However, when we sin, it crushes the Spirit. Therefore, the spirit of the Spirit is crushed every time we sin. This is a very important point for believers to comprehend. The more we engage in sinful activity, the more we crush the Spirit of God. Continuous sin prevents the Spirit from taking over our lives. As a matter of fact, the flesh becomes the ruler of our lives while the Spirit of God becomes restricted. As a result, we end up with strongholds and habits that become extremely hard to deal with.

THE REMODELED PREMISES

We don't want to grieve the Spirit. We should desire to be filled by Him because He is **the reliable source** for us to depend on when dealing with others. He is the resource we rely on in order to deal with difficult people. He can keep us from turning to sin, if we totally surrender to Him. Paul gives us some examples in Ephesians 4:31, when he says, "Let all bitterness, and wrath, and anger, and clamor, and evil speaking, be put away from you, with all malice."

The Holy Spirit can help us with **the residing resentment** we have toward others. The word *bitterness* means "sharp resentment." Every time a person sees or thinks about a person who has offended him, it reaches the very core of that person's existence. When bitterness goes unchecked, it grows and takes root in us. Therefore, we need the Holy Spirit presiding over our lives in order to prevent resentment from residing in our lives.

Without leaning on the prevailing power of the Holy Spirit, the sharp resentment gives way to wrath. The word *wrath* deals with **the retaliation rendered** when someone has offended us. It is the idea of doing unto others as they have done unto you. When the Holy Spirit is not controlling us, wrath becomes an automatic reaction from the victim offended. The reciprocated response of fighting fire with fire will always grieve the Holy Spirit. When the flesh is in control, reciprocation and retaliation will be planted in your heart and mind by Satan to get even with the one that offended you.

Let's address **the recognized root** of the problem. We need to recognize the root of the resentment and retaliation. It is anger.

If we do not address anger properly, these things will happen. We have already discussed the fact that anger is not a sin but it can lead to sin (see Ephesians 4:26). However, anger cannot be harnessed without receiving help from the Holy Spirit.

If we don't allow the Spirit to take over when we are wronged by others, **the released rage** automatically surfaces. If we don't deal with anger properly, clamor surfaces. The word *clamor* deals with arguing, brawling, and quarreling. A shouting match will surface as a result of the Holy Spirit not being in control.

You would never raise your fist against your offender or curse him out. However, when you say things to others about the offender, it can lead to **the ruined reputation**. This is what evil speaking and malice infer in Ephesians 4:31. You may never brawl with the individual, but slandering his name and speaking evil about the person is just as destructive. The use of slanderous and hurtful speech does not flow from the lips of a person filled with the Holy Spirit.

THE RIGHTEOUSNESS PRACTICED

As believers, we are members of **the caring family**. Paul said, "And be ye kind one to another" (Ephesians 4:32a). The word *kind* means to be caring and courteous. I remember staying with my grandparents as a kid with other cousins one summer. Something happened to cause me to get in a fight with my cousin Regina. My grandmother sent us in the house while she removed a switch from what we called, "the switch tree." Yes, she used the switch on us but the moment is memorable because of what she said to us. With tears in her eyes, she said, "You need to be kind to one another because you are kin."

Paul was basically saying the same thing as Grandma. "Be kind to all, especially your kinfolk." In Romans 12:10, Paul says, "Be kindly affectioned one to another with brotherly love; in honour preferring one another." As brothers and sisters in the Lord, we should love one another.

Love is an action word. A lot of people will say, "I love you," but never show it. Paul says, we are to be "kind one to another" (Ephesians 4:32a). Kindness deals with **the commended favor** shown toward others. When one is kind, he shows and showers favor on others. Instead of fighting, we are to shower with favor. After Jesus met with Peter following the resurrection, he asked Peter repeatedly if he loved Him. Each time Peter responded by telling Jesus that he loved Him. After Peter's response each time, Jesus told him to show it by "feeding His flock" (see John 21:15-17).

As a believer, you should be considered **the compassionate friend** of others. This is what Paul is referring to when he uses the word *tenderhearted* in Ephesians 4:32. The word means to be full of compassion, understanding, love, and warmth. It means to be aware of a person's hurts and sufferings, problems and difficulties. It carries the idea of befriending another. A true friend shows compassion according to his or her knowledge of the other person.

Next Paul talks about **the commanded forgiveness**. He says, "Forgiving one another, even as God for Christ's sake hath forgiven you" (Ephesians 4:32). Forgiveness means to pardon a person for some wrong done. It involves being gracious to a person who has offended you and others. "To forgive or not to forgive" is not a question. Throughout the Bible, the subject of forgiveness is always treated as a command rather than a consideration. We are to forgive one another. How can a person move beyond the hurt and pain caused by the offender and forgive? The power to forgive is linked to the Holy Spirit in our lives. Whatever God has commanded us to do, the Holy Spirit helps us to do it.

If you need a motivation to be kind and to forgive others, think about **the caring Father** in our lives. We are to forgive even as God has forgiven us for Christ's sake. The offenses committed against us pale in comparison to what we have done against God. Yet God has forgiven us. We rebelled against God but He still chose to forgive us. God forgives us no matter what we have done. Therefore, this should motivate us to forgive.

I can imagine someone reading this information and saying, "I hear what you are saying but I'm not God." I know, but the there is another point to pull from this command. Every time you think about not forgiving someone, **the created flashbacks** should cause you to go through with the command to forgive. Think about what you have done and what God forgave you of.

Paul says that we have been forgiven "for Christ's sake" (see Ephesians 4:32). Christ is responsible for **the covered faults** of believers. The greatest act of forgiveness occurred on a hill called Calvary when Jesus died for the sins of the world. As a result of the death of Christ, every fault has been covered with the blood of Christ and we have been forgiven for it. Since Christ has forgiven us, we should forgive others. In Colossians 3:13, Paul says, "Forbearing one another, and forgiving one another, if any man have a quarrel against any: even as Christ forgave you, so also do ye."

Chapter 15

FOLLOWING THE RIGHT LEADER
EPHESIANS 5:1-7

The Faithful Church
The Claimed Belief
The Connected Body
The Copied Behavior
The Christian Brand
The Constant Battle
The Children Born

The First Child
The Saint's Steps
The Substitutionary Sacrifice
The Same Standard
The Sweet Smell
The Son's Submission
The Stated Satisfaction

The Follower's Conduct
The Frequent Temptations
The Flesh Tamed
The Fleeing Tempter
The Foul Temple
The Filthy Tongue
The Foolish Talking
The Flowing Thankfulness

The Fallen Company
The Damnable Practices
The Doom Pronounced
The Deceptive People
The Distorted Precepts
The Decided Punishment
The Disapproved Partnership

IF YOU ARE a committed follower of the Lord, the world will know it. The light cannot be hidden. On the other hand, if you are pretending, the world will eventually discover this as well.

Years ago, I noticed the flower bed at a house in the distance as I drove my son to school. It was beautiful and I wanted my flower bed to stand out just like it. I purchased flowers that looked similar to the ones I saw in the distance at the home near my son's school. I tried everything possible to make my flowers look the same, but Texas heat prevented it from happening. One day, I saw the homeowner in the yard after I dropped my son off for school and decided to go up and get horticulture tips from her. As I drove closer to the flowerbed, I discovered why her flowers looked great from a distance. They were fake flowers made of plastic.

If you get close enough, you will learn that there are a lot of fake followers pretending to be who they are not.

THE FAITHFUL CHURCH

In Ephesians 5:1, Paul says, "Be ye therefore followers of God, as dear children." This message reveals that **the claimed belief** does not automatically mean that a person is saved. Having religion does not mean that a person has a relationship with the Lord. Salvation cannot happen without engaging the heart. The Lord told us that many will claim to believe and approach Him at the end and He will tell them that He does not know them. Jesus said, "But he shall say, I tell you, I know ye not whence ye are; depart from me, all ye workers of iniquity" (Luke 13:27).

Note the word *be* in the passage. This deals with **the connected body**. It means "to become" attached to God. The believer must be attached or connected to God to be saved. The claim without the connection is worthless. Jesus Christ is the divine connector. He said, "I am the way, the truth, and the life: no man cometh unto the Father, but by me" (John 14:6). There is no other way to become attached to God except by Jesus Christ.

It is the claimed belief and **the copied behavior** that authenticate our relationship with God. The word *follower* means "to imitate."

We are to become imitators of God. The true claim and connection will be seen in the conduct. We are told repeatedly to be like God. Jesus said, "Be ye therefore perfect, even as your Father which is in heaven is perfect" (Matthew 5:48). Peter said, "But as he which called you is holy, so be ye holy in all manner of conversation; because it is written, Be holy; for I am holy" (1 Peter 1:15-16).

Let's not forget that we were purchased by God. He is the owner. In a sense, we have been branded to prove ownership. Your behavior serves as **the Christian brand** in your life. Your behavior reveals that you have been bought with a price. Periodically, I hear people say, "You must be a Christian." The comment is usually made because of something I said or did. In 1 Corinthians 6:19-20, Paul says, "What? Know ye not that your body is the temple of the Holy Ghost which is in you, which ye have of God, and ye are not your own? For ye are bought with a price: therefore glorify God in your body, and in your spirit, which are God's."

As mentioned before, there is **the constant battle** taking place between the flesh and the Spirit in our lives. As we shall see in just a moment, following God gives us the victory in this battle. As a result of this ongoing battle, we must work hard daily to live in a way that pleases the Lord. Satan will attempt to lure us away from truth and righteousness. Therefore, we must crucify the flesh daily so that we will not allow the enemy to draw us away. Don't forget that God always provides an escape when the tempter seeks to trap us (see 1 Corinthians 10:13).

Paul said that we are to be followers of God as "dear little children" (see Ephesians 5:1). Paul uses a great example with **the children born** to us. When our children are born into this world, they learn by imitating us. As parents, we are our children's first teachers and pastors. They not only learn from what they hear us say but also by what they see us do. Since our children learn from us, we must serve as great role models for them to follow. Just as our children imitate us, we are to imitate our heavenly Father.

THE FIRST CHILD

Paul says that **the saint's steps** should give him away every time. He said, "And walk in love, as Christ also loved us, and hath given himself for us an offering and a sacrifice to God for a sweetsmelling savour" (Ephesians 5:2). The saint's steps are saturated in love. It is the walk of love that authenticates our genuine connection to Jesus Christ. When we are committed to God, we will walk in love. Jesus said, "By this shall all men know that ye are my disciples, if ye have love one to another" (John 13:35). This unconditional love proves that we are His disciples.

The phrase "gave himself for us" in Ephesians 5:2 points to **the substitutionary sacrifice** that made salvation possible. It has a simple but significant meaning. What it means is that Christ died in our place, in our stead, as our substitute. We were dead and scheduled to die a couple of more times (physical and the second death) but God provided the ultimate sacrifice. Jesus said, "I am the good shepherd: the good shepherd giveth his life for the sheep" (John 10:11). He also said, "As the Father knoweth me, even so know I the Father: and I lay down my life for the sheep" (John 10:15). "Greater love hath no man than this, that a man lay down his life for his friends" (John 15:13).

Paul is also informing us that **the same standard** of sacrifice is required of every believer. The phrase "gave himself for us" does not mean that Christ died only as an example for us, showing us how we should be willing to die for the truth or for some great cause. No, you don't have to die on a cross to prove your commitment to God. We should become the living sacrifices witnessing to the world by showing love one to another.

Paul deals with **the sweet smell** of the sacrifice. He gave Himself for us an offering and sacrifice to God for a sweet-smelling savor (smell). The words *offering* and *sacrifice* refer to the burnt offering of the Old Testament. The burnt offering was not given to God to merely address sin; it was offered to glorify God. The action was taken to figuratively create a sweet smell in the nostrils of God. Therefore, it could not have been offered for sin only because sin stinks. When we live for Christ and love like Christ, it is like that sweet-smelling sacrifice.

The sweet smell came as a result of **the Son's submission.** Jesus' ultimate goal was to please His Father. He submitted to His will instead of His own. His submission did not always line up with the religious establishment, which often led to conflict. Jesus went about seeking to please and glorify God at all times. It was about truth rather than tradition or trends. When we surrender and submit as saints, we glorify God.

The submission of the Savior led to **the stated satisfaction.** God spoke repeatedly during Jesus' earthly ministry (baptism and transfiguration) and said, "This is my beloved Son in whom I am well pleased." We need to hear God say, "This is my beloved child in whom I am well pleased." When we submit to God and become faithful stewards, He will be satisfied. In Matthew 25, the parable of the talents, Jesus said, "His lord said unto him, Well done, thou good and faithful servant: thou hast been faithful over a few things, I will make thee ruler over many things: enter thou into the joy of the Lord" (Matthew 25:21).

THE FOLLOWER'S CONDUCT

When you choose Christ, you should expect to deal with **the frequent temptations.** As you follow Christ, you should expect temptations to surface. As mentioned before, the purpose is to entice and lure you in a different direction. You are trying to follow God and the enemy tries to pull you away.

When we submit to the Spirit's power, we end up seeing **the flesh tamed.** As you follow Christ, the flesh is not taken away but tamed. Early on in the relationship, I was slipping and sliding all over the place. As I matured in Christ, the flesh stopped winning. The Spirit of God helped me to be victorious. In the past, the devil didn't have to do too much to entice me.

Early on, the devil used to hang out with me. However, when I really committed to follow Christ, I witnessed **the fleeing tempter** more and more. You win by submitting yourself to God first. As a result of submitting to God, you receive power to resist the devil. As a result, he flees from you. "Submit yourselves therefore to God. Resist the devil, and he will flee from you" (James 4:7).

Next Paul addresses **the foul temple.** Paul says, "But fornication, and all uncleanness, or covetousness, let it not be once named among you, as becometh saints; Neither filthiness, nor foolish talking, nor jesting, which are not convenient: but rather giving of thanks" (Ephesians 5:3-4). We are to be morally pure (clean-bodied). The believer seeks to keep his body free of fornication, uncleanness, and covetousness. They are not to be named among you. When Paul says that they should not be named among us, he is telling us that we should not even talk about these acts (in the sense of engaging in them). In 1 Timothy 5:22, Paul says, "Neither be partaker of other men's sins: keep thyself pure."

Once again, Paul comments on **the filthy tongue.** The believer following God is not only to be clean-bodied but clean-mouthed as well. If a believer is to follow and imitate God, he has to be pure in speech and conversation. The believer is never to be engaged in filthiness: using the mouth in obscene, shameful, polluted, immoral conduct and conversation. In Titus 2:8, Paul says, "Sound speech, that cannot be condemned; that he that is of the contrary part may be ashamed, having no evil thing to say of you."

Okay, you are not guilty of having a filthy tongue but **the foolish talking** and jesting is wrong as well. Foolish talking is empty, senseless, or purposeless talk that does nothing but waste time. It also means sinful and corrupt talk. Jesting is to poke fun and make wisecracks. Note that such talk is not convenient, fitting, or becoming to believers. "A fool uttereth all his mind: but a wise man keepeth it in till afterward" (Proverbs 29:11). Peter says, "For he that will love life and see good days, let him refrain his tongue from evil, and his lips that they speak no guile" (1 Peter 3:10). Paul says, "Let your speech be always with grace, seasoned with salt, that ye may know how ye ought to answer every man" (Colossians 4:6).

The above mentioned conduct is not becoming but **the flowing thankfulness** from the mouths of believers is commendable. Paul says, "which are not convenient: but rather giving of thanks" (Ephesians 5:4). Believers are to be engaged in conversations that build people up and offer thanks and praise to God. When you do this extensively, you will not have time for the others. In Colossians, he says, "And whatsoever ye do in word or deed, do all in the name of the Lord Jesus, giving thanks to God and the Father by him" (Colossians 3:17). He also says, "In everything give thanks: for this is the will of God in Christ Jesus concerning you" (1 Thessalonians 5:18).

THE FALLEN COMPANY

The damnable practices listed in Ephesians 5:5 are not designed to be a full list of sins to avoid. Paul simply uses the list of sins as an example of why the unregenerate man cannot spend eternity with God. Paul said, "For this ye know, that no whoremonger, nor unclean person, nor covetous man, who is an idolater, hath any inheritance in the kingdom of Christ and of God" (Ephesians 5:5). To expand on the meaning here, "No whoremonger (*pornos*: illicit sexual intercourse; fornication, prostitution), nor unclean person (*akathartos*: immoral, contaminated, dirty thoughts or behavior), nor covetous man (*pleonexia*: coveting, craving, desire to have what others have) who is an idolator (*eidololatreia*: the worship of idols). . . . " It is not about what one professes but what one practices.

The person living and practicing these sins will not share in the kingdom of God. And note, **the doom pronounced** is not just related to the future. It is also connected to the present. It does not say, "He shall not have," but rather, "he does not have an inheritance with God." There is still an opportunity for him to have a place in the kingdom if he repents and surrenders his life over to the Lord.

Beware of **the deceptive people** using a lot of religious rhetoric. Paul says, "Let no man deceive you with vain words" (Ephesians 5:6). I mentioned in one of the earlier chapters that Paul wrote this letter when the philosophy of Gnosticism had slipped into the church. The Gnostic said that man is both body and spirit but the spirit was the only important part of man—the only part that really matters. It is the part that really concerns God. They believed it didn't matter what a man did with his body. The Word teaches that Jesus is interested in the whole man.

There are deceivers walking about us. They disguise themselves to be godly when they are not. In 2 Corinthians 11:13-14, Paul speaks of the disguise when he says, "For such are false apostles, deceitful workers, transforming themselves into the apostles of Christ. And no marvel; for Satan himself is transformed into an angel of light."

Many have become confused by **the distorted precepts** presented by false prophets. These deceivers will try to dilute and distort the principles and precepts of God's Word. They will say, "If you are saved by grace and not by works, you can live any way you desire." These deceivers with the distorted precepts will tell you things like: "Since sex is normal and natural, it is okay to sleep around with whomever you desire whenever you desire." They will deceive you into thinking it is okay to desire to be sexually attracted to and involved with the same sex since God made you that way. In Romans, Paul says, "For they that are such serve not our Lord Jesus Christ, but their own belly; and by good words and fair speeches deceive the hearts of the simple" (Romans 16:18).

The decided punishment has already been declared by God. Paul says, "For because of these things cometh the wrath of God upon the children of disobedience" (Ephesians 5:6). The decisive anger (wrath) of God rises and stands against this wickedness. If there is no change, the wrath of God will come upon them. In Romans 1:18, Paul says, "For the wrath of God is revealed from heaven against all ungodliness and unrighteousness of men, who hold the truth in unrighteousness."

Paul concludes this section by addressing **the disapproved partnership** with those behaving ungodly. Paul says, "Be not ye therefore partakers with them" (Ephesians 5:7). We are directed to separate ourselves from the unclean. Believers are not to participate in their sin nor hang out with the ones doing it. In 2 Corinthians 6:14, Paul says, "Be ye not unequally yoked together with unbelievers: for what fellowship hath righteousness with unrighteousness? and what communion hath light with darkness?" If we are presently partnering with them, Paul says, "Now we command you, brethren, in the name of our Lord Jesus Christ, that ye withdraw yourselves from every brother that walketh disorderly, and not after the tradition which he received of us" (2 Thessalonians 3:6).

SHINE ON ME
EPHESIANS 5:8-14

WHILE HEADED TO our midweek service at the church where I serve as pastor, we witnessed a power outage in the Dallas area where the church is located. As I drove to the church, I noticed that it was pitch black in the neighborhood near the church and you could only see the lights on the cars driving up and down the road. As I turned the corner, to my surprise, the church was lit up and glowing. No, it wasn't due to divine intervention that the church was aglow. When the power outage occurred, the backup generator automatically kicked on. Yes, there was darkness in the city but the church was shining brightly.

We live in a dark world but the light of Jesus should cause the church (the body of believers) to shine in the midst of the darkness.

Throughout this epistle, Paul has addressed **the dark past** of all believers. He says, "For ye were sometimes darkness" (Ephesians 5:8). We haven't always been saved and full of the Holy Spirit. Before a person is saved, he is not only in darkness, but he *is* darkness. It simply means that the person is apart or separated from God (the Light). His whole life is shadowed and covered with darkness.

The dark past is always a reference to **the disobedience practiced.** The dark past means that all of us were disobedient people, behaving based on the sinful nature in us. We were not living according to the original divine nature in which man was created. In Genesis, God said, "Let us make man in our image, after our likeness . . . " (Genesis 1:26a). We know that light is connected to His image because when we go to heaven, we will not need a sun to shine because God's presence will light the city. The sin in the garden produced the darkness.

Due to the dark past, we deserved to die. **The death penalty** was the ultimate sentence. Due to the presence of darkness (sin), humanity was destined to die and to be eternally separated from God. The punishment started with Adam and Eve being dismissed from the presence of God (the source of light). They could no longer stay around the light due to sin. They had to immediately be separated from the Father of Lights (see James 1:17). As a result, we were all destined to die from the beginning of our existence. As a matter of fact, when we were born physically, we were spiritually DOA.

Check out **the different profile** we have since Jesus came into our lives. Paul said, "For ye were sometimes darkness, *but now are ye light* in the Lord" (Ephesians 5:8, emphasis added). We were once darkness but we have become light. Instead of being labeled darkness, we are now identified as light in the Lord. The best way to explain this spiritual phenomenon is to look at the moon. The moon glows but does not shine. The moonlight is "lit up" due to the reflection from the sun that we do not see. Therefore, the moon is glowing at night because of the sunlight. Like the moon, the believer's light is just a reflection of the Son.

We are light because of **the deliverance provided** through our Lord and Savior Jesus Christ. We have been delivered by the Light of the world. He brought us out of darkness and placed us in His marvelous light. How did this happen? John says, "In him was life; and the life was the light of men" (John 1:4). Paul says, "Who hath delivered us from the power of darkness, and hath translated us into the kingdom of his dear Son" (Colossians 1:13). Jesus made it possible for us to glow.

It is worth noting again that the deliverance provided represents **the debt paid** for our sins. He provided the deliverance by paying the debt that no one else could pay. In John 1, we see Jesus described as the light of men. John bore witness of the Light (John 1:7), who was the true Light (1:9), which came to light men. How did He do it? It took the death of the Light to deliver us from the darkness of death.

The disciple's path should be bright because he is walking in the light. Since we are now light in the Lord, we should walk as children of light (see Ephesians 5:8). We should walk as people of light and not people of darkness. We are described as *children of light*. In 1 Thessalonians 5:5, Paul uses the same description when he says, "Ye are all the children of light, and the children of the day: we are not of the night, nor of darkness." As children, we are the offspring of our heavenly Father. James describes Him as the Father of lights when he says, "Every good gift and every perfect gift is from above, and cometh down from the Father of lights" (James 1:17). When we are not walking like the Light, it dishonors the one who begot us, the Father of lights.

Look at what else the Father of lights did for us. He provided **the dependable power** to help us do what He has commanded of us. Paul said, "For the fruit of the Spirit is in all goodness, and righteousness, and truth" (Ephesians 5:9). He not only gave His Son as the ultimate sacrifice, He gave us His Spirit as the power source to help us do what He demands of us. It is impossible to shine without Him.

Although the Holy Spirit is dependable, **the disciplined partner** learns to submit to His power. He will never force us to do anything. We have already discussed the importance of being filled with the Spirit rather than merely being satisfied with the indwelling of the Spirit. If He simply dwells in your life, the light will be dull and dim. In a sense, the wattage of your light is determined by how much control you give the Spirit of God in your life. God desires for us to be 100-watt believers but it can't happen without being full of the Holy Spirit.

Look at **the divine principles** linked to the dependable power within us. When the Holy Spirit presides over our lives, goodness, righteousness, and truth become the by-products. In Ephesians 5:9, Paul says, "For the fruit of the Spirit is in all goodness [full of virtue], and righteousness [to be right and do right], and truth [opposite of a lie and hypocrisy]." Jesus repeatedly describes the Holy Spirit as the Spirit of truth (see John 14:17; 15:26; 16:13). When the truth reigns in your life, goodness and righteousness come.

The definitive proof of our righteousness comes as we walk in the light. As we walk in the light, "*we prove what is acceptable unto the Lord*" (Ephesians 5:10, emphasis added). This verse simply means that the light proves things. The light causes us to see what is good and what is bad. In the dark, everything looks the same, but the light allows us to see the good and the bad. In 1 Thessalonians 5:21, Paul says, "Prove all things; hold fast that which is good."

Don't be fooled by **the disguised participants** who are children of darkness with masks on. We have already dealt with the deceivers in our midst and how Satan disguises himself as an angel of light. Paul said, "For such are false apostles, deceitful workers, transforming themselves into the apostles of Christ. And no marvel; for Satan himself is transformed into an angel of light" (2 Corinthians 11:13-14). These disguised participants are good performers (fooling the very elect). However, the separation of the wheat and tares will happen in the future.

The dividing partition should be placed between the children of light and the children of darkness. Once again, we are told not to fellowship with the unfruitful works of darkness (Ephesians 5:11a). We discussed the unfruitful works in the last chapter. Paul simply revisits the subject to let us know that we should not be found fellowshipping with people participating in evil and unfruitful works of sin. When God saved us, He called us out of that lifestyle.

At the end of Ephesians 5:11, Paul says, "But rather reprove them." **The duty performed** before departing or separating from them is extremely important. Before we separate ourselves from the unfruitful workers of darkness, we should reprove them. The fellowship with unfruitful works of darkness is strictly forbidden, but we have the responsibility to reprove (expose, rebuke, and convict) people of their sins or dark works. Jesus said, "Take heed to yourselves: If thy brother trespass against thee, rebuke him; and if he repent forgive him" (Luke 17:3). In 2 Timothy 4:2, Paul says, "Preach the word; be instant in season, out of season; reprove, rebuke, exhort with all long suffering and doctrine."

Paul says, "For it is a shame even to speak of those things which are done of them in secret" (Ephesians 5:12). It sounds like Paul is contradicting his last statement here. He has just instructed us to reprove them but now says that it is a shame to speak of those things which are done of them in secret. **The disgraceful procedure** is connected to the last two words of verse twelve. It is a shame to speak of the evil "in secret." Paul is saying that we need to stop talking to people about the sins of others in secret. We need to go directly to the worker of unfruitful works and reprove him.

Paul says, "But all things that are reproved are made manifest by the light: for whatsoever doth make manifest is light" (Ephesians 5:13). My presence as a believer will affect **the dim places** around me. When you (the light) go to reprove the sinner, you (the light) step into a dim or dark place but you (the light) dispel the darkness due to your presence. Your light can touch the lives of those in darkness so they can see the way out.

Paul says, "Wherefore he saith, Awake thou that sleepest, and arise from the dead, and Christ shall give thee light" (Ephesians 5:14). At first glance, I thought Paul was dealing with **the disconnected people** in this verse. It is true that the unsaved person is not connected to the Lord but Paul is not dealing with unsaved people here. This letter was written to believers in Ephesus. If people (the plug) are disconnected to the power source, it is impossible to shine.

You can be plugged in and still be disconnected to the power source due to **the detached pole**. Let me explain with this illustration. One day, I moved a lamp from the family room to the garage where I have a desk. Several weeks passed before I tried to turn the light on. When I did, I discovered that it didn't work.

I checked to see if it was plugged in and it was. I then checked the bulb to make sure it had not blown out and it hadn't. I plugged something else into the socket to make sure the outlet worked and it did. I was about to trash the lamp when I noticed a portion of the cord cut and discovered that it didn't work due to the detached electric wire. In the plug, the wire had been cut and the power could not flow through it. I had to split the covering, twist the wires, and cover it again with electrical tape. I plugged it in and turned the knob and it came on.

We need to: Wake Up! Look Up! Get Up! Stand Up! Step Up! Speak Up! When we do these things, we will Light Up the world!

Chapter 17

THE PROOF IS IN THE PUDDING
EPHESIANS 5:15-21

The Strict Walk
The Steps Watched
The Savior's Witnesses
The Sinner's Worldliness
The Sinister Weights
The Saint's Wisdom
The Spiritual Warfare
The Shown Way
The Seconds Wasted
The Society's Wickedness

The Savior's Will
The Scriptures Written
The Strong Wine
The Sober Walker
The Spirit Working
The Serious Worshipper
The Special Weapon
The Senseless Worrying
The Submissive Worker

YOU CAN TELL me that your pudding tastes great. You can list the various ingredients and talk about special steps taken to blend everything together. You can talk about how you used slow, even strokes as you whipped it into the wonderful pudding that is. However, I will not agree or disagree with you until I taste the pudding. In other words, the proof is in the pudding.

Paul says, "See then that ye walk circumspectly, not as fools, but as wise" (Ephesians 5:15). **The strict walk** is demanded of the believer. We are to walk circumspectly (*akribos*). The word *circumspectly* means carefully and accurately—to be exact. The strict walk should be modeled after Jesus Christ. In Colossians, Paul says, "As ye have therefore received Christ Jesus the Lord, so walk ye in him" (Colossians 2:6). John says, "He that saith he abideth in him ought himself also so to walk, even as he walked" (1 John 2:6).

Let me comment on **the steps watched** by others. When we walk circumspectly, we must watch our steps and realize that others are watching. A good man's steps are ordered by the Lord. We watch our steps to make sure they line up with His orders. The places where we walk should be lit up when we travel there. As we walk, we should shine in this world. Jesus said, "Ye are the light of the world. A city that is set on a hill cannot be hid" (Matthew 5:14). John says, "But if we walk in the light, as he is in the light, we have fellowship one with another, and the blood of Jesus Christ his Son cleanseth us from sin" (1 John 1:7).

As we walk, we must remember that we are **the Savior's witnesses**. We also realize that others are watching our steps and many will desire to know Jesus as a result of our witness. We should strive to be strong and solid witnesses for the kingdom at all times. We shine so that people will see Jesus when they look in our direction. Jesus also said, "Let your light so shine before men, that they may see your good works, and glorify your Father which is in heaven" (Matthew 5:16).

Believers are not to get up in **the sinner's worldliness**. We are to walk circumspectly and not as fools (see Ephesians 5:15). This is what is meant by the phrase "not as fools." It is the fool that says in his heart there is no God. The foolish or unwise walker is the person who is thoughtless, careless, uncaring, and worldly-minded. The psalmist had them in mind when he told us not to do what they do. The psalmist said, "Blessed is the man that walketh not in the counsel of the ungodly, nor standeth in the way of sinners, nor sitteth in the seat of the scornful" (Psalm 1:1).

Before boasting about not being fools, we need to start with the main reason why we are not. We have been washed by the blood of the Lamb. We have not arrived. One day, the Spirit of God convicted our hearts and we received the gift of salvation. John said, "But if we walk in the light, as he is in the light, we have fellowship one with another, and the blood of Jesus Christ his Son cleanseth us from all sin" (1 John 1:7).

We cannot walk in holiness without addressing **the sinister weights** in our lives. If you are walking or running for Jesus, you must put away certain things. The writer of Hebrews dealt with this one. He said, "Wherefore, seeing we also are compassed about with so great a cloud of witnesses, let us lay aside every weight, and the sin which doth so easily beset us, and let us run with patience the race that is set before us, Looking unto Jesus the author and finisher of our faith" (Hebrews 12:1-2a).

We are to be wise in our walk as we walk circumspectly, not as fools (see Ephesians 5:15). **The saint's wisdom** (*sophia*) comes from God. The wise person is the one that is the spiritually-minded person. He has a personal relationship with the Lord and desires to walk according to His commands. He delights in the law of the Lord and meditates on it day and night (see Psalm 1:2). The wise believer seeks God with his whole heart and keeps His testimonies (see Psalm 119:2). He constantly reviews his walk and turns his feet according to God's Word (see Psalm 119:59-60).

The wise saint understands that **the spiritual warfare** is real. I will deal with this topic in detail when we get to Ephesians 6, but it is worth mentioning now. Satan desires to cause you to stumble. As you try to walk circumspectly as a wise believer, the path will offer many exits and detours. Satan will try to entice and lure us in an attempt to pull us off of the divine path. This is why we need to be wise as we travel on this path. We should be wise enough to recognize his schemes. In 2 Corinthians 2:11, Paul says, "Lest Satan should get an advantage of us: for we are not ignorant of his devices."

Satan looks for the weaknesses and places of vulnerability in our lives. I have some good news and some bad news for you. First, the bad news is that you cannot handle the temptations of the devil. The good news is that God will show you the way out. The shown way is the door of escape. Paul says, "There hath no temptation taken you but such as is common to man: but God is faithful, who will not suffer you to be tempted above that ye are able; but will with the temptation also make a way to escape, that ye may be able to bear it" (1 Corinthians 10:13).

The wise one will "redeem the time" (see Ephesians 5:16). This deals with the seconds wasted in this life. Paul is not talking about buying time. You have already received the gift of time from God. He is talking about using your time wisely. Don't waste it. One thing I know I've done wrong is that I stayed a sinner much too long. Now I need to use every second I have to work the works of Him who sent me while it is day for the night is coming (when time will be no more). Every second that ticks by is a reminder that it is getting late in the evening and the sun is going down on us. The psalmist says, "So teach us to number our days, that we may apply our hearts unto wisdom" (Psalm 90:12).

We need to redeem the time because of the society's wickedness. Paul said that "the days are evil" (Ephesians 5:16). The days are filled with wickedness. We are living in a sin-sick society. Believers are confronted with evil on a daily basis. The evil days will not end until the Lord returns for the church. Therefore, we must redeem the time by taking every opportunity to shine for Christ and share the good news about Christ. Paul says, "Walk in wisdom toward them that are without, redeeming the time" (Colossians 4:5).

Paul says, "Wherefore be ye not unwise, *but understanding what the will of the Lord is*" (Ephesians 5:17, emphasis added). We are not to be unwise. We are to seek to understand **the Savior's will.** The word *understand* means to grasp, perceive, and comprehend. If the believer does not seek to understand what the will of the Lord is, he ends up acting like the unwise and foolish person discussed earlier. The psalmist said, "I delight to do thy will, O my God: yea, thy law is within my heart" (Psalm 40:8).

It probably goes without saying that **the Scriptures written** must be studied in order to understand what the will of the Lord is. He has given us the Bible. He has supplied the Scriptures for us to learn His will. We must read the Bible rigorously. When Satan tempted Jesus in the wilderness, He dealt with each temptation by reciting the Word of God (see Luke 4:1-13). It is important to note that Jesus didn't simply recite the Scriptures, He rehearsed the Scriptures. Paul says, "All scripture is given by inspiration of God, and is profitable for doctrine, for reproof, for correction, for instruction in righteousness" (2 Timothy 3:16).

Paul says, "And be not drunk with wine, wherein is excess" (Ephesians 5:18). **The strong wine** would be equivalent to what we would call a "stiff drink." Drunkenness means to be intoxicated with drink or drugs that can lead to excessive behavior. The verse does not say, "Don't drink in excess" as some use this text to explain their drinking habit. The passage is dealing with the mind-altering intoxicant that can lead to uncontrolled behavior. Drunkenness distorts reality and gives the devil the advantage over us.

On the other hand, **the sober walker** can face the attacks of the enemy better. As we walk, we can only walk in victory when we are sober. We are to be sober and vigilant. Peter says, "But the end of all things is at hand: be ye therefore sober, and watch unto prayer" (1 Peter 4:7). He also says, "Be sober, be vigilant; because your adversary the devil, as a roaring lion, walketh about, seeking whom he may devour" (1 Peter 5:8). When we are attentive and alert, we can focus on the will of the Lord and walk accordingly.

The sober walker must have **the Spirit working** in order to be victorious on this journey. Paul says, "And be not drunk with wine, wherein is excess; *but be filled with the Spirit*" (Ephesians 5:18, emphasis added). We can know the will of the Lord when we allow the Spirit to work in our lives. Instead of being drunk with wine, we should be filled with the Spirit. Paul says, "This I say then, Walk in the Spirit, and ye shall not fulfil the lust of the flesh" (Galatians 5:16).

Next Paul deals with **the serious worshipper.** He says, "Speaking to yourselves in psalms and hymns and spiritual songs, singing and making melody in your heart to the Lord; giving thanks always for all things unto God and the Father in the name of our Lord Jesus Christ" (Ephesians 5:19-20). Paul has just instructed the believer not to be drunk with wine that leads to excessive behavior. Instead of being full of wine, he tells us to be filled with the Holy Spirit. Now Paul tells us how to worship. These two verses give a beautiful description of private and public worship. The serious worshipper engages in speaking Scripture, singing songs, praying, and praising.

Before leaving this point, I have to deal with Paul's directives from another angle. In a real sense, Paul is showing the difference between being under the influence of spirits (wine) and being drunk in and under the influence of the Holy Spirit. When you are drunk with wine, it affects your walking. When you are under the influence of the Spirit, you don't walk like you used to walk. Have you ever paid attention to a person intoxicated by alcohol or drugs being on an emotional high due to the substance in their system? They laugh, sing, and smile like they don't have a care in the world (at least until the hangover comes). When we are under the influence of the Holy Spirit, we end up on a spiritual high and the good news is that we can stay there.

At the end of Ephesians 5:20, Paul says that the believer should be "giving thanks always for all things unto God and the Father in the name of our Lord Jesus Christ." This verse deals with a couple of important points. It deals with **the special weapon** of praise. When we learn to bless the Lord at all times, Satan knows he is in trouble. Since God inhabits the praises of His people (see Psalm 22:3), the devil knows the powerful presence of God in our lives will prevent him from winning. Therefore, we should always give God thanks for all things.

It also deals with **the senseless worrying** over life's issues. We are to give thanks always for all things. This includes the things that we don't understand as well as the difficult times we face on this journey. Why should we give thanks for all things? Paul says, "And we know all things work together for good to them that love God, to them who are called according to his purpose" (Romans 8:28).

Paul concludes this section by dealing with **the submissive workers**. In Ephesians 5:21, he says, "Submitting yourselves one to another in the fear of God." In this verse, Paul is sharing how to prevent division and disunity in the church. When a Spirit-filled believer has a submissive, respectful spirit, it is hard to find bickering and quarreling. Instead of a spirit of dissension and divisiveness existing in the church, there should be a spirit of submission in which all believers respect and honor other believers in the fear of the Lord. When we submit to one another, it carries the idea of going out of your way to minister and serve.

The proof is in the pudding. You are either a wise walker or a foolish one.

Chapter 18

GOD'S WORD ON MARRIAGE
EPHESIANS 5:21-33

THE STARTING POINT

PAUL ADDRESSES THE subject of marriage in this portion of the letter to the Ephesians. In Mark 10, the Pharisees came to Jesus to ask a question about divorce. They said, "Is it lawful for a man to put away his wife?" (see Mark 10:2). Matthew adds, "for every cause" (Matthew 19:3). There was a background to this question. The societal influence of Jesus' day was very loose morally—even the Jewish society.

Marriage was considered no more than a business transaction on a piece of paper: If it worked, fine; if it didn't work, divorce. They asked about divorce but Jesus gave them an answer about marriage (see Mark 10:5-9). Why would Jesus respond with a message about marriage rather than divorce? It was primarily due to the fact that the institution of marriage had been de-emphasized while divorce was prioritized in that society. That mindset really hadn't changed much in Paul's day (or our day), so he was inspired by God to address the matter in this letter.

When dealing with the subject of marriage, it is important to view it as **the spiritual institution** established by God. In the book of Genesis, God instituted marriage when He created Eve for Adam. As an institution established by God, it must operate according to His divine design in order for it to work as He intended. Since marriage is a spiritual and sacred institution ordained by God, we cannot change the original blueprint even though we live in a different day and time.

It goes without saying that all institutions established by God will come under attack by the enemy. He will influence people to go against what God has ordained. **The satanic influence** has invaded all of the institutions of God (family, marriage, church, etc.) and attempted to destroy what God created. The divorce rate is at an all-time high because of this satanic invasion. This why Jesus said, "In the beginning it was not so" (Matthew 19:8).

The satanic influence will always lead to **the sinful interpretation** by many. Satan's influence is seen when people seek to alter God's original design to fit their fleshly desires. The open marriage concept embraced by some married couples is a perfect example of the sinful interpretation. Another example would be the acceptance of same-sex marriages. God designed marriage to take place between a man and a woman. Yes, God intended for a man (male) and a woman (female) to come together and unite in holy matrimony. Therefore, same sex unions violate the biblical description of marriage.

The divine law should always override the civil law. The law of the Lord should be prioritized over the laws of the land. The Supreme Court of the land can endorse same-sex marriages in society, but their opinion does not make it right. No man has the right or authority to change what God has ordained.

Let me comment on **the saved individuals** united in holy matrimony. Ideally, the institution established by God works best when you have a saved man and a saved woman involved. Husbands and wives are to be equally yoked. Any single man or woman planning to marry one day should verify the spiritual state of the one interested in you. Don't be satisfied with the claim; check out the conduct. Jesus said, "Wherefore by their fruits ye shall know them" (Matthew 7:20).

The institutions established by God will not function properly without applying **the Scriptural instructions** from the Lord. People will attempt to twist the truth of God Word. For instance, they will tell you that the scriptures related to marriage should not be viewed from a "gender" perspective. They claim that the Bible is about love and if a man loves another man or a woman loves another woman, this ideology lines up with the overall message of the Bible.

They will tell you that the historical context must be considered in comparison to the contemporary situation. In other words, they believe the change of times means that the biblical view should be changed to support their desires. In Romans, Paul says, "Wherefore God also gave them up to uncleanness, through the lusts of their own hearts, to dishonour their own bodies between themselves: Who changed the truth of God into a lie" (Romans 1:24-25).

The Scriptural instructions don't mean much without **the Spirit's involvement**. Before dealing with the practical matters related to marriage, family, and employment in Ephesians chapters five and six, Paul said, "And be not drunk with wine, wherein is excess; but be filled with the Spirit" (Ephesians 5:18). The Spirit of God empowers us to do what God requires from us. The marriage made in heaven cannot work properly without the Spirit of God controlling the husband and wife.

THE SUBMISSION PRINCIPLE

Let's take a look at **the divine assignment** given to wives in Ephesians 5:22 and Colossians 3:18. Paul says, "Wives, submit yourselves unto your own husbands." The wife is to walk in a spirit of submission according to the Word of God. This is not an assignment created by a man. God commands the wife to submit to the leadership of her husband.

By the way, there is not a qualifier connected to the submission. The verse does not say that the wife is to submit to her Christian husband. I have heard Christian women say that they would submit if their husbands were spiritual men. Peter said, "Likewise, ye wives, be in subjection to your own husbands; that, if any obey not the word, they also may without the word be won by the conversation of the wives" (1 Peter 3:1).

She is to submit to her own husband, *as unto the Lord* (see Ephesians 5:22, emphasis added). The submission commanded deals with **the disciple's accountability** to Christ. She loves the Lord; therefore, to please Him she submits herself to her husband. It is done out of love of and loyalty to the Lord and her husband. A true disciple of Christ does not pick and choose which commands she will obey. In a real sense, the wife's submission to her husband authenticates her commitment and submission to the Lord. She realizes that she must give an account to the Lord when she fails to follow His commands.

Let me comment on **the difficult adjustment** some wives have submitting to their own husbands. It is difficult for some women to make the adjustment because they have lived independently for a long time before the husband came into her life. This is also true when it comes to our relationship with the Lord. Before we surrendered our lives to the Lord, the flesh controlled us. After becoming saved, we had to learn how to crucify the flesh daily because it continued to try to govern us. The same is true for the wife releasing her independence after marriage. It takes time to adjust after operating another way for so long.

In some cases, there is a need for **the dismissed attitude** that comes with the submission. The submission should be done without a negative attitude attached. It is like the wife who said to her husband, "I am only submitting to you because the Bible told me to do it but I don't really want to submit." This attitude dishonors God and the husband. We should follow the instructions of God simply because it is right to do so.

The husband is **the delegated authority** in the marriage. Paul said, "For the husband is the head of the wife. . . . " The word *head* in Scripture refers to authority. Neither man nor woman is superior to the other person. Men and women are equal in God's eyes. In 1 Corinthians 11:11-12, Paul says, "Nevertheless neither is the man without the woman, neither the woman without the man, in the Lord. For as the woman is of the man, even so is the man also by the woman; but all things of God." In Galatians, Paul says, "There is neither Jew nor Greek, there is neither bond or free, there is neither male or female: for ye are all one in Christ Jesus" (Galatians 3:28).

If neither is superior, why should the wife submit? It is **the designated arrangement** according to the Word of God. Since it does not mean that women are inferior to men, what does it mean? It simply means that there is to be an arrangement, an order in the household. You cannot have two heads in any organization. The designated arrangement was first mentioned in the book of

Genesis. The writer says, "Unto the woman he said, I will greatly multiply thy sorrow and thy conception; in sorrow thou shalt bring forth children; and thy desire shall be to thy husband, and he shall rule over thee" (Genesis 3:16).

Paul deals with **the direct association** between the wife's submission to her husband and the church's submission to Christ. Paul says, "Even as Christ is the head of the church: and he is the saviour of the body. Therefore as the church is subject unto Christ, so let the wives be to their own husbands in every thing" (Ephesians 5:23-24). The wife's submission is compared to Christ and the church. As she submits to Christ, so she is to submit to her own husband. As she depends upon Christ for help and protection, so she is to depend upon her husband for help and protection. As she depends upon Christ for companionship and comfort, so she is to depend upon her husband for companionship and comfort.

Before discussing the husband's role, let me address **the dangerous actions** that wives need to be aware of. The first dangerous action deals with the wife's submission that is on one minute and off the next. She is to submit in everything (as long as it is not sinful). The second dangerous action is switching roles and responsibilities. Don't think you can switch the order because you make more money or because you believe you are smarter than your husband. You may even be more spiritual than your husband, but you have not been authorized to become the head.

THE SUPERVISORY POSITION

Paul says, "For the husband is the head of the wife, even as Christ is the head of the church: and he is the saviour of the body" (Ephesians 5:23). As we deal with the husband as the head, let's address **the misunderstood status**. When God talks about man being the head of the woman, He is not talking about ability or worth, competence or value, brilliance or advantage. God is talking about function and order within the organization.

Although the husband is designated as the head, we must not overlook **the mutual submission** commanded in the Word of God. The starting point for the marriage discussion should not be Ephesians 5:22. It should be Ephesians 5:21, "Submitting yourselves one to another in the fear of God." When there is mutual submission, the husband and wife will honor and respect one another. Peter says, "Likewise, ye husbands, dwell with them according to knowledge, giving honour unto the wife, as unto the weaker vessel, and as being heirs together of the grace of life; that your prayers be not hindered" (1 Peter 3:7).

Let's look at **the main subject** attached to the husband's role. Paul says, "*Husbands love your wives* even as Christ also loved the church, and gave himself for it" (Ephesians 5:25, emphasis added). The husband's role is covered with *agape*. It is commanded for the husband to love his wife. Once again, we don't see a qualifier. The verse does not say, "Husbands love your wives when they are submissive." We tend to think about love in terms of emotions. However, the word *agape* refers to love as a principle and not an emotion. There is the emotional word for love (*phileo*). There is also the physical love (*eros*). Paul is dealing with unconditional love.

Next we have **the mirrored Savior** attached to this subject. We are to love our wives even as Christ also loved the church and gave Himself for it. Husbands are to mirror the Savior's love. Think about Christ's love for the church here. He gave Himself for it. This is a sacrificial love. In Romans 5:8, Paul says, "But God commendeth his love toward us, in that, while we were yet sinners, Christ died for us." He loved us when we were not lovable. As husbands, we must follow the Lord's example.

The mission statement for the husband is recorded next. He gave Himself for the church "that he might sanctify and cleanse it with the washing of water by the word, That he might present it to himself a glorious church, not having spot, or wrinkle, or any such thing; but that it should be holy and without blemish" (Ephesians 5:26-27). The love that Christ has for the church transforms her. We are great at seeing blemishes, spots, wrinkles, faults, and failures. However, the love of Christ looks beyond who we are to what He is transforming us to become.

Paul said, "So ought men to love their wives as their own bodies. He that loveth his wife loveth himself. For no man ever yet hated his own flesh; but nourisheth and cherisheth it, even as the Lord the church" (Ephesians 5:28-29). A person who yells at himself, cursing himself out, beats on himself would be labeled as **the mentally sick**. A man should love his wife the way he loves himself. Most well-adjusted people love themselves. The word *cherish* means to hold ever so dear and to treat with warmth due to value and worth. The word *nourish* means to feed, clothe, provide for, nurture, and look after. You cherish and nourish your body because you love it. Husbands should cherish and nourish their wives the same way. Paul says that husbands should nourish and cherish their wives "even as the Lord the church" (see Ephesians 5:29). The Lord views the church as His bride. He promised never to leave or forsake the church (see Hebrews 13:5).

The church is not only His bride, it is His body. In Ephesians 5:30, Paul deals with **the membership status** of all believers. Paul said, "We are members of his body, of his flesh, and of his bones." A believer is a member of His body. The church body is connected to Him. As a matter of fact, this connection causes us to have life and to have it more abundantly (see John 10:10). Each member of a body shares the same life source. It is controlled by the same spirit, washed by the same blood, and ruled by the same brain.

Next Paul deals with **the matrimonial step** taken by the couple. Paul said, "For this cause shall a man leave his father and mother, and shall be joined unto his wife, and they two shall be one flesh" (Ephesians 5:31). To be joined means to cleave to or be glued together. It carries the idea of being completely absorbed and assimilated into each other. In marriage, two people become one person. Have you ever paid attention to the name given to the first married couple? After God married Adam and Eve, check out the name he gave them. In Genesis 5:2, the writer says, "Male and female created he them; and blessed them, and called their name Adam, in the day when they were created." These were two people with one name.

Paul identifies marriage as **the mysterious symbol** as it relates to the church. Paul says, "This is a great mystery: but I speak concerning Christ and the church" (Ephesians 5:32). When people see a marriage made in heaven, they also see the great mystery of Christ and the church. All of the elements of marriage are seen in the church (submission, sacrifice, love, etc.).

At the end of Ephesians 5, we have **the message summarized**. Paul summarizes the subject matter by saying, "Nevertheless, let every one of you in particular so love his wife even as himself; and the wife see that she reverence her husband" (Ephesians 5:33). The husband is to love his wife unconditionally and the wife is to reverence her husband, which means to put him on a pedestal and speak well of him. By the way, if the husband loves his wife unconditionally, the submission and reverence are made easier for the wife.

Chapter 19

CHILD CARE NEEDED
EPHESIANS 6:1-4

The Child's Holiness
The Charged Headship
The Christian Home
The Creator's Help
The Church Huddle
The Caregivers Honored
The Coming Harvest
The Continued Heritage
The Created Hellion
The Constant Hypocrisy
The Constraining Hedge

The Conduct Harnessed
The Considered History
The Complete Honesty
The Correction Handled
The Cushioned Hindquarter
The Costly Hesitation
The Creative Hardship
The Caring Heart
The Critical Heartache
The Clinging Hope

I TOOK THIS title from an email I received from a member of the church where I serve. In the subject line of the email, it said "Child Care Needed." A parent who had recently relocated from the West Coast and united with our church wanted to know if I could recommend a place that provided quality child-care services.

In this passage, Paul begins this chapter by saying, "Children, obey your parents in the Lord; for this is right" (Ephesians 6:1).

Let's start with **the child's holiness**. The phrase implies an act of holiness or righteousness based on the performance of the child. Our children are expected to be holy. It is the right thing to do. In Colossians 3:20, Paul said, "Children, obey your parents in all things: for this is well pleasing unto the Lord." Children please the Lord when they honor and obey their parents.

This verse also reveals **the charged headship** of parents. The word *obey* means to submit to; to comply with; to heed; to follow the directions or guidance of instructions. In the last chapter, we dealt with the headship of the husband in the marital relationship. Now Paul deals with the headship of the parents when it comes to rearing children. The father and mother have been given the charge to rule their children. The writer of Proverbs 1 says, "My son, hear the instruction of thy father, and forsake not the law of thy mother; for they shall be an ornament of grace unto thy head, and chains about thy neck" (Proverbs 1:8-9). Our primary responsibility is to parent our children and not to try to become their best friends.

It goes without saying that **the Christian home** is pictured here. The phrase "in the Lord" points to a child being in a right relationship with the Lord. It also implies that the child is being raised in a Christian home or environment. However, a child born in a Christian home does not come into that home as a Christian but as a sinner. Children have to be "born again" in order to be in the Lord. It is the responsibility of parents to steer them in this direction.

The charge to bring up our children in a spiritual way requires **the Creator's help**. I believe every parent will agree that raising children is more than a notion. We really don't have to look at our children to reach this conclusion. If we reflect on our days as children, we can remember days when we didn't always behave as the holy offspring of God-fearing parents. Yes, we all challenged our parents' child-rearing skills. It is challenging to rear children but with the help of the Lord, it can be done.

I struggle with the saying, "It takes a village to raise a child." The reason I struggle with it is because I don't want everyone in the village involved with raising my children. Now I do believe in **the church huddle** taking place to assist with childrearing. I do believe parents and children need to be involved in the church. When we attend church, it is like in football getting into a huddle to review the plays to run in order to receive the victory. Yes, the "no huddle" offense is okay at times, but you need to huddle periodically to make sure everyone is on the same page. When you have other God-fearing people on the team with you, it can help with the task of raising the children the right way.

Now Paul deals with **the caregivers honored** by the children. He says, "Honor thy father and mother; which is the first commandment with promise" (Ephesians 6:2). The word *honor* (*timao*) means to "esteem and value as precious." It means to show respect and reverence. Parents are dishonored when children talk back, ignore, disregard instructions, speak disrespectfully, etc. Whenever I observe children yelling and cursing out their parents, it grieves me. This is sinful and can lead to destruction. In Proverbs 20:20, the writer says, "Whoso curseth his father or his mother, his lamp shall be put out in obscure darkness." The cutting eyes of disrespect and the disregard of parental instruction are just as bad as cursing out a parent. In Proverbs 30:17, the writer says, "The eye that mocketh at his father, and despiseth to obey his mother, the ravens of the valley shall pick it out, and the young eagles shall eat it."

There is **the coming harvest** as a result of children obeying and honoring their parents. As the first commandment with promise, obedient children can expect a harvest. He says, "That it may be well with thee, and thou mayest live long on the earth" (Ephesians 6:3). A child who grows up to love, honor, and obey his parents has a harvest coming. Things will go well for the child. This does not mean the child will never have problems. It means God will be with the child to strengthen and take care of him.

The child is assured that he will live a long life on earth. Yes, there are exceptions when God chooses to call a precious little life to be with Him earlier than we expected. The main point of the passage is that the child's life will not end early due to walking the unrighteous path.

The long life leads to **the continued heritage** or tradition passed down from generation to generation. As a result of our children being raised in a holy atmosphere, it will most likely continue to future generations. After the children of Israel crossed over the Jordan in the book of Joshua, the people were instructed to stack the stones they took from the bottom of the Jordan. In Joshua 4:21, Joshua said, "When your children shall ask their fathers in time to come, saying, What mean these stones?" The parents were to tell the children what the Lord did for them so they could learn about God as well as learn to lean on Him in the future. This is how the Christian heritage continues as well.

Paul gives a stern warning to fathers (really fathers and mothers). He warns against **the created hellion** as a result of the action or inaction of the adults in the child's life. In Ephesians 6:4, Paul says, "And ye fathers, provoke not your children to wrath." The word *provoke* means to arouse to wrath or anger, to provoke to the point of utter resentment. In Colossians 3:21, Paul said, "Fathers, provoke not your children to anger, lest they be discouraged."

We should never be guilty of causing our children to engage in sin due to our actions. Over-controlling or under-controlling a child can provoke a child. When we neglect our responsibility to raise them properly, it can lead to their destruction. The writer of Proverbs 22 says, "He that soweth iniquity shall reap vanity: and the rod of his anger shall fail" (Proverbs 22:8).

Let me go back to the commandment given to children in the first verse. Children are commanded to obey their parents *in the Lord* (see Ephesians 6:1, emphasis added). When a parent offers a command "not in the Lord," the child is not required to obey. The Lord has nothing whatsoever to do with the filth of unrighteousness and abuse of precious children. Jesus said, "And whosoever shall offend one of these little ones that believe in me, it is better for him that a millstone were hanged about his neck, and he were cast into the sea" (Mark 9:42).

We also provoke our children with **the constant hypocrisy** they see in our lives. Living an inconsistent life before a child can provoke a child. A parent that tells a child one thing and turns around and does the opposite is full of hypocrisy. The same inconsistency will probably be displayed in the child's life when he grows up. Repeatedly in the Old Testament we hear these words: "And he did evil in the sight of the Lord, and walked in the way of his father, and in the way of his mother (1 Kings 22:52). The apple doesn't fall that far from the tree.

We need **the constraining hedge** in place to properly bring up our children in the nurture and admonition of the Lord. This hedge serves as a protective measure. We must keep them in and keep others out for a season. It is my belief that the home is supposed to be the true headquarters of "Child Protective Services." We cannot leave our children to raise themselves. The writer of Proverbs 29 says, "The rod and reproof give wisdom: but a child left to himself brings his mother to shame" (Proverbs 29:15).

We cannot bring them up in the nurture and admonition of the Lord without keeping **the conduct harnessed** or controlled. Our children are born as sinners just as we were. You don't have to teach a child to lie or misbehave because the sinful nature is in them from birth. As parents, we must address sinful behavior in our children immediately to keep strongholds from being formed in their lives. When we discipline our children, it is designed to help instead of hurt them in the long run. The writer of Proverbs 23 says, "Thou shalt beat him with the rod, and shalt deliver his soul from hell" (Proverbs 23:14).

As we discipline our children, I believe **the considered history** should always be viewed by the parents. It is sad that we soon forget that we were once children living in the flesh rather than living in the Spirit. We often view the defiant behavior of our children as an incurable disease that will exist forever. As I watched my boys grow up, I often saw a lot of their father (me) in them. I had done some of the "bad things" that I saw them doing. This served as a reminder that the same God who delivered me from the error of my ways could do the same for them.

Since I just mentioned the parents' history, let me comment on **the complete honesty** about the journey that must be shared with our children. Our children often view us as angelic beings that have always been the way we are. They need to know that we messed up in the past. It is okay for parents to be transparent with their children. As a matter of fact, when we own up to our past failures, it often gives our children hope for future success in life.

As a child is brought up, we must discipline him or her when the behavior is defiant rather than compliant. The parent is the primary one responsible for **the correction handled** when the child misbehaves. The writer of Proverbs 22 says, "Foolishness is bound in the heart of a child; but the rod of correction shall drive it far from him" (Proverbs 22:15). Defiance must be confronted early or it will blossom into full-fledged rebellion.

Most child-rearing experts believe that the basic values and behavior systems are set in their children by their sixth birthday. Discipline must take place through every stage of your son or daughter's physical development (infancy, toddler, early childhood, and adolescent stages). Don't skip those stages and think that you can get him right as a teenager. The age to begin is not a chronological one but rather when you see the seeds of willful defiance to authority beginning to germinate in their hearts. Even the toddler slapping mom on the face should not be seen as something cute.

We live in a time in which spanking is considered child abuse. However, the Bible has authorized this form of discipline. It can be done because of **the cushioned hindquarter** of the child. The writer of Proverbs 23 says, "Withhold not correction from the child: for if thou beatest him with the rod, he shall not die" (Proverbs 23:13). God has provided a padded posterior of the anatomy which can receive mildly painful corrective measures without harming a child. God never intended for you to wrap thorns around a switch or use a hot iron to discipline your child. These actions are evil and I believe this type of corporal punishment should lead to the parent being jailed.

Let me comment on **the costly hesitation** when it comes to not taking care of the discipline required. I cannot overemphasize the importance of parents addressing disobedience immediately. When our children know they will not suffer consequences from doing that which is evil, we end up creating a problem for others. For instance, the behavior in the classroom will give the teacher the blues because the child has been permitted to get away with evil behavior at home. In Proverbs 19:18a, the writer says, "Chasten [discipline] thy son while there is hope." The writer of Proverbs 13 says, "He that spares his rod hates his son; but he that loves him chastens [disciplines] him betimes [promptly]" (Proverbs 13:24).

I need to comment on **the creative hardship** at this point. Hardship can help to create productive citizens. Many parents were reared in homes in which the parents were strict disciplinarians. I have heard parents say that because they had strict parents, they do not want their children to go through similar hardship as they witnessed as children. I struggle with this view because of how they turned out in life. As a result of the discipline they witnessed, they ended up being successful in life. The creative hardship helped them to stay on the straight and narrow path.

The child should know that the chastisement is flowing from **the caring heart** of the parent. God loves His children too much not to discipline us when we are wrong. The writer of Proverbs 3 says, "My son, despise not the chastening of the Lord; neither be weary of his correction: for whom the Lord loveth he correcteth; even as a father the son in whom he delighteth" (Proverbs 3:11-12). There are times when this act of love is not appreciated until later in life. Discipline is not something we do "to" our children but something we do "for" our children. We must get to the point that we love our children too much to allow them to practice destructive patterns of behavior.

Since I just commented on the caring heart, let me deal with **the critical heartache** caused by defiant children. Satan knows that the God-fearing parent grieves when his children are not behaving properly. The very core of the parent is crushed. I can remember one of the disciplinary days as a fourteen-year-old child when my mom used the "swinging switch" on me. As painful as the experience was to me, I witnessed something later on that was much more painful. When I heard my mom crying and praying in her room over my behavior, it changed my life forever. By the way, I have been preaching since I was fifteen.

Let me conclude this lesson by dealing with **the clinging hope** that we must have as parents. I don't care how defiant a child may be, we should never give up on the possibility of change in that child's life. It's not too late for the power of God to prevail in the life of any child. One of my older sisters used to say, "If our children can be full of hell, they can also be filled with the Holy Spirit." If you have done your part, you should cling to hope for your child or children.

SLAVES AND MASTERS
EPHESIANS 6:5-9

YOU RARELY HEAR pastors deliver sermons from passages like this one recorded in Ephesians 6:5-9. If you hear a message from the passage, the emphasis is usually placed on employer/employee relations. I am in agreement with this emphasis to a certain degree. Like most theologians, I will view the text from this angle in this chapter. However, I cannot overlook a subject that must be addressed when dealing with Ephesians 6:5-9. The subject matter is slavery.

THE WITNESSED ERA

Paul says, "Servants, be obedient to them that are your masters according to the flesh, with fear and trembling, in singleness of your heart, as unto Christ" (Ephesians 6:5). The Greek word translated "servants" here is *slave*. The subject of slavery was one of **the challenging topics** to be addressed by Paul and others in the Scripture. Pastors often bypass this passage because it is a challenging subject to deal with. The topic of slavery is still a sensitive matter in our time. However, we cannot deny the fact that there have been eras in the history of the world in which slavery was prominent. From the surface, it appears as though the passage supports and endorses this evil practice that existed in society.

When studying the Word of God, **the considered times** of the writing will help to properly interpret the passage. Vast numbers of people (including members of the Gentile church) were slaves in the Roman Empire. It is estimated that there were over sixty million slaves in the Roman Empire during the days of Paul. They didn't have any civil rights and they were bought and sold like animals. They were considered pieces of property. This letter was written long before America was discovered and slave ships sailed to Africa. There was a slave revolt led by Spartacus that led to much bloodshed.

I don't believe anyone reading this book would endorse slavery. However, isn't it interesting that you don't read about **the condemned transgression** of slavery the Bible? It is interesting that the Bible does not come right out and condemn slavery. Neither does the Bible formally approve slavery. Although the Bible does not come out and directly condemn slavery, it speaks volumes about loving one another and treating people right. The Bible does not tell us not to abuse our spouses or not to molest children, but the other principles and precepts of Scripture cause us to know this is wrong.

In the book of Exodus, we see God's objection to the system of slavery instituted by Pharaoh. God did not send Moses to just lead the children of Israel to the Promised Land. He sent Moses to deliver His people from **the cruel taskmasters**. When Jacob and his descendants first arrived in Egypt, they were treated like citizens. After Joseph and the pharaoh died, the Israelites ended up becoming slaves.

I believe **the coming testimony** had something to do with the Bible not addressing the condemnation of this evil system in society. In every generation, there were abolitionists to rise up and preach against slavery. God knew that the people would one day receive truth and change the system throughout the world. God has always raised a person like Moses to say, "Let my people go!" It is great that the days of slavery are gone from most of the world.

Before moving on, I must comment on **the clever teaching** of former slave owners as it relates to the Scripture. Centuries later, after slavery was institutionalized in America, the slave owners did not want their slaves educated. They would teach portions of the Scripture to make them think they were spiritually obligated to obey. For instance, they would teach them about Ephesians 6:5-8 but leave out the information recorded in Ephesians 6:9 that involved the master treating the slave right. They would teach Colossians 3:22 that deals with slaves obeying in all things but leave out the discussion of Colossians 4:1 that instructs slave owners to be just and treat slaves as equals. They would teach from 1 Timothy 6:1 and fail to mention 1 Timothy 6:2.

It is great to know that the laws have finally changed and institutionalized slavery has been abolished in most places in the world. However, we are not completely out of the wilderness.

You still have **the concealed thoughts** of some people supporting the ideology of slavery. Unfortunately, we still have people with the mindset that some people are not equal with them. Therefore, racism still exists and I honestly don't think it will end until there is a new heaven and a new earth.

There are hate groups that continue to poison and program the minds of people. In the United States, the debate over the Confederate flag is a perfect example. When men want to fight over their heritage without admitting to the hatred connected to the heritage, there is something seriously wrong.

THE WORKMAN'S ETHICS

Now let's deal with the behavior of the employees and employers. I believe this section of Ephesians can be applied to the workplace. Let's start with **the followed laws.** The workman is to follow the laws of the employer. Paul said, "Servants, be obedient to them that are your masters according to the flesh" (Ephesians 6:5). The workman is to obey; that is, he is to follow the rules and instructions of the employer. Note the phrase "according to the flesh." It deals with the physical realm (not the spiritual) and implies that the employer has authority over the employee.

The feared Lord will cause people to follow the laws. The Christian workman is to work with fear and trembling. This is not the fear of man but the fear of God in your heart. The Christian employee must be afraid of disobeying the Lord. You are on the job for Jesus. The work ethic of the Christian worker should be above reproach.

Next the employee is to be seen as **the focused laborer.** The Christian workman is to work in "singleness of heart" as to Christ (see Ephesians 6:5). This means that the laborer should work with focused attention, in sincerity and without any pretense or hypocrisy. There is no pretense and the worker desires to do a good job at all times. Please note that his service is being offered to the Lord and not to the business or corporation. The Christian employee embraces excellence.

"Singleness of heart" also deals with **the full load** of the worker. It deals with each worker doing his or her part to reach the desired goal. If one is not carrying his load, it will have an effect on the others and their loads carried. Therefore, the worker is not to call in sick when he is healthy. He is not to conduct personal business on the clock. He is not to spend the day surfing through the internet and posting on Facebook. He is not to arrive late and leave early.

The forbidden laziness is also implied here. You should not find the focused laborer frequently lounging on the job. The Christian employee is not to work with eye-service as a man-pleaser. He is not to work just when the employer or boss is looking. The Christian workman is not to impress the employer when he is around and slack off when he is out of sight. The compensation received should be earned from working hard at all times. Let me revisit a passage addressed earlier in this book. In Ephesians 4:28a, Paul said, "Let him that stole steal no more: but rather let him labor, working with his hands the thing which is good." The command is to stop stealing and to find a job. However, if you find a job and don't work as expected, you are actually stealing.

The Christian employee always has **the Father looking** at his performance. The Christian worker must remember that he is a servant of Christ doing the will of God from the heart (Ephesians 6:6b). Therefore, it does not matter whether the work is secular or sacred. The Father has His eyes on us. The employer who is a Christian is working for the Lord. The Lord is the true manager. All of us are in ministry. It doesn't matter if you are a dispatcher or deacon; plumber or preacher, economist or evangelist, policeman or pastor, mechanic or missionary; you are to focus on doing the will of God. All of these vocations are in God's will and must be done from the heart.

When it comes to **the fellow's loyalty** as an employee, the primary goal is not to just perform well for a promotion or a pay raise. Paul says, "With good will doing service, as to the Lord, and not to men" (Ephesians 6:7). Our loyalty to the Lord should be prioritized. We are to fulfill our job responsibilities to please the Lord. By the way, when we are loyal to Him, all of the other things are added.

Paul says, "Knowing that whatsoever good thing any man doeth, the same shall he receive of the Lord, whether he be bond or free" (Ephesians 6:8). This deals with **the future lot** of the Christian employee. There is no respect of persons with God. You will reap based on what you have sown. By the way, you may not get everything you deserve on this side for working hard. Don't worry. God will bless you in the future.

THE WARNED EMPLOYERS

The same bylaws exist for the employer. Paul says, "And, ye masters, do the same things unto them" (Ephesians 6:9). Basically, Paul is saying, "Do unto others as you would have them do unto you." The employer, manager, or supervisor is to do the same things that are required of the employee. The Holy Spirit reminds the employer of his obligations and responsibilities. They have rules to follow as well. If you expect a fair day's work, you must give a fair day's pay.

It is great when **the supervisor's beliefs** line up with the Word of God. Although the passage implies that the supervisor believes in the Lord as well, we cannot always choose to work for a company in which God reigns in the life of the owner. In this case, the workman is still required to be faithful and focused. In some cases, God can use the Christian workman to draw the unbelieving employer to the Lord. A perfect example of this can be found in the book of Genesis with the character by the name of Joseph. The Joseph story reveals that your spiritual state can cause things to change in the workplace. With all of the non-believing Egyptians Joseph worked for, they all saw the Lord as a result of Joseph's work ethic (see Genesis 39:3; 39:23; 41:38).

Paul said, "And, ye masters, do the same things unto them, forbearing threatening" (Ephesians 6:9a). In a real sense, this is dealing with **the servants bullied** or harassed by their employers. Love, not force or fear, is the best way to encourage people to work. When the supervisor believes, he will not seek to burden the servants employed but try to work with them to a certain point. When employees know they are valued and appreciated, they will work harder and better. Employers should never become mean and malicious taskmasters.

Let me comment on **the scheduled bankruptcy** for the employer abusing the employees. Over the years, I have seen countless business enterprises fold or file bankruptcy because of the ungodly treatment of employees and customers. The business that chooses to mistreat employees will not last long. The bankruptcy scheduled for the future is inevitable. The business can't keep employees and as a result the "going out of business sign" goes up. The psalmist said, "Fret not thyself because of evildoers, neither be thou envious against the workers of iniquity. For they shall soon be cut down like the grass, and wither as the green herb" (Psalm 37:1-2).

Paul is not speaking against **the stern boss** in this passage. Just in case you are thinking that a Christian employer should never threaten to terminate an employee, let me tell you that you are sadly mistaken. This phrase does not mean the spiritual boss should not be stern when it comes to correcting an employee and possibly releasing that employee. God does not encourage slothfulness and indulgence. Just as God disciplines when needed, the employer must do the same with his employees. If the job performance is always below standard, the employer must be stern with the employee.

It is possible for **the successful business** with a spiritual boss to suffer when employers ignore the bad employees in the midst. When the employer refuses to deal with the bad apples in the bunch, it can lead to the other apples eventually going bad. When the boss fails to be stern with love, the other employees will be affected. By the way, the church staff is included here. When the employer fails to deal with the bad apples, it will lead to **the staff blues.** The morale of the staff is also affected when the uncommitted employee remains on the staff. This does not mean the other employees will not perform well. They will do their jobs but dislike the environment in which they are required to work daily. They talk in the break room about the other employees receiving pay for a poor job performance. They talk about how unfair it is for them to work hard while the other employee barely shows up to work.

Let me comment on **the shared bounty** next. When the employer realizes that the business is blessed because of having God-fearing employees on board, he will share his bounty. The Lord rewards us believers for our faithfulness. Employers should do the same. When a business is thriving as a result of having hardworking employees, promotions, pay raises, and bonuses should be considered. This also causes the employee to work even harder at his job.

Paul concludes this section by commenting on **the sinful bias** of employers. He says, "Knowing that your Master also is in heaven; neither is there respect of persons with him" (Ephesians 6:9b). The employer and the employee must remember that we have a Master in heaven and He has no favorites and shows no favoritism. God sits high and looks low. He is watching us and holding all of us accountable.

Chapter 21

ARMED AND DANGEROUS
EPHESIANS 6:10-24

The Constant Warfare
The Addressed Saints
The Amazing Strength
The Accessible Source
The Armed Soldiers
The Attacks Scheduled
The Active Spirits
The Allowed Strikes
The Ammo Supplied
The Army Standing

The Christian's Weaponry
The Received Truth
The Righteous Team
The Ready Troop
The Regiment's Training
The Real Test

The Redemptive Terms
The Renegade's Target
The Renewed Thoughts
The Recorded Testaments
The Rear Tackle

The Concluding Words
The Serious Praying
The Specific Petition
The Spirit's Participation
The Saint's Perseverance
The Strengthened Preacher
The Sibling Present
The Sacred Profession
The Salutation Proclaimed
The Sincere Practice
The Solemn Postlude

PICTURE THIS. SATAN meets with his demons to dispatch them to attack the saints of God. He calls your name and says, "I need one of my most powerful demons on this mission because he is armed and dangerous."

THE CONSTANT WARFARE

Let's start this last chapter with **the addressed saints** that this letter is written to. In Ephesians 6:10, he says, "Finally, my brethren . . . " Paul is speaking to the saints of God. Therefore, the charge that he is about to give is to Christian believers who belong to Jesus Christ. It is not a directive given to people in the world or worldly people in the church. He is addressing blood-bought born-again believers.

He deals with **the amazing strength** of all believers. He said, "Be strong in the Lord, and in the power of his might" (Ephesians 6:10). The Christian believer must be strong in the Lord and in the power of His might. The strength and power is designed to help us stick to the fight when we are hardest hit. It is strength and power to hold on and hold out. In Colossians, he says, "Strengthened with all might, according to his glorious power, unto all patience and longsuffering with joyfulness" (Colossians 1:11). In Ephesians 3:20, he has already said, "Now unto him that is able to do exceeding abundantly above all that we ask or think, according to the power that worketh in us."

The accessible source of our strength is Jesus Himself. We are to be strong *in the Lord* and in the power of *His* might. Jesus Christ is the source of our strength. We are in Christ and He is in us. Therefore, we have strength and power through Him. In Isaiah, the prophet said, "Fear thou not; for I am with thee: be not dismayed; for I am thy God: I will strengthen thee; yea, I will help thee; yea, I will uphold thee with the right hand of my righteousness" (Isaiah 41:10).

By the way, you cannot be victorious relying on your own might, power, and strength. Also, His strength is made perfect in our weakness. You don't have to live in fear because Paul said,

"For God hath not given us the spirit of fear; but of power, and of love, and of a sound mind" (2 Timothy 1:7).

We must put on the whole armor of God (Ephesians 6:11a). When Christ saved us, He called us to become **the armed soldiers** in His army. We have to pull off the old man and put on the new. We are believers who are to be armed and ready. In 2 Timothy 2:3-4, Paul says, "Thou therefore endure hardness, as a good soldier of Jesus Christ. No man that warreth entangleth himself with the affairs of this life; that he may please him who hath chosen him to be a soldier." The Lord is our Commander and we are on the battlefield for Him.

We need to be armed soldiers due to **the attacks scheduled**. All of this should be done so that we may be able to stand against the wiles of the devil (see Ephesians 6:11b). The word *wiles* means deceits, methods, and strategies. Paul says, "Lest Satan should get an advantage of us: for we are not ignorant of his devices" (2 Corinthians 2:11). Peter says, "Be sober, be vigilant; because your adversary the devil, as a roaring lion, walketh about, seeking whom he may devour" (1 Peter 5:8). The moment you surrendered your life to the Lord, you were placed on the devil's hit list. He is out to get you.

With the attacks scheduled, Paul makes it clear that the warfare is not human or physical. Paul says, "For we wrestle not against flesh and blood, but against principalities, against powers, against the rulers of the darkness of this world, against spiritual wickedness in high places" (Ephesians 6:12). Paul is dealing with **the active spirits** commanded and ruled by Satan. The word *wrestle* is an athletic term. It is a contest between opponents. The forces of evil are powerful and numerous.

They rule the darkness. Darkness is a reference to one's ignorance of truth. They are spiritual forces of wickedness. They are after the spirit of man destined and created to worship and serve God. It is true that the warfare is not against humans or physical (flesh and blood) but these evil forces or spirits will often reside in human bodies.

The allowed strikes seem to be unfair when you are seeking to serve the Lord. It should be understood that God permits the enemy to strike. Yes, He has the power to prevent it from happening but chooses to allow the strikes to come. The reasons vary. 1) Some strikes are allowed to "grow" us. You will never know how to use your power without being attacked at times. 2) He uses strikes to humble us. Paul said, "And lest I should be exalted above measure through the abundance of the revelations, there was given to me a thorn in the flesh, the messenger of Satan to buffet me, lest I should be exalted above measure" (2 Corinthians 12:7). 3) He allows the strikes to remind us that we are not in heaven yet.

How do you deal with the strikes? You are to take **the ammunition supplied** to fight against the enemy. In Ephesians 6:13, he basically repeats the command that he has already given in Ephesians 6:11. He says, "Wherefore take unto you the whole armour of God, that ye may be able to withstand in the evil day, and having done all, to stand" (Ephesians 6:13). When is the evil day in this verse? It is today and any day with the onslaught of evil we see happening around us. The evil days have existed every day since Satan was kicked out of heaven.

Since we do not wrestle against flesh and blood, we need a different type of arsenal to combat principalities, powers, rulers of darkness, and spiritual wickedness in high places. You fight against principalities and powers with a higher principality and greater power. You combat darkness with light. You combat spiritual wickedness with spiritual righteousness. In 2 Corinthians 10:4, Paul says, "For the weapons of our warfare are not carnal, but mighty through God to the pulling down of strong holds."

The victory for the Christian soldier has nothing to do with destroying the enemy. The goal is to keep **the army standing**. It is also important to see that the objective is to be able to "stand" against the wiles of the devil. We will not defeat the devil in the truest sense of the word. God will take care of that one day. Until that day comes, Christians are to stand. Since the Lord has commanded us to stand, He has equipped us to do it.

THE CHRISTIAN'S WEAPONRY

Next Paul deals with the specific weaponry at our disposal. The first weapon deals with **the received truth**. He says, "Standing therefore, having your loins girt about with truth" (Ephesians 6:14). The Roman soldier's belt or girdle held the armor in place and protected the lower portion of the soldier's body. Truth is the first piece of armor we must put on.

Satan is the father of lies and we need to use truth to combat him. When Jesus came, Truth arrived. He came that we would know the truth and be set free by it. John says, "And the Word was made flesh, and dwelt among us, (and we beheld his glory, the glory of the only begotten of the Father,) full of grace and truth" (John 1:14). Later in John, Jesus says, "I am the way, the truth, and the life: no man cometh unto the Father, but by me" (John 14:6).

The next piece of armor reveals God's army as **the righteous team**. Paul says, "And having on the breastplate of righteousness" (Ephesians 6:14). The breastplate of the Roman soldier protected the upper portion of his body from the neck to the thighs. The most vital organ of the human body, the heart, was protected. The writer of Proverbs 4:23 says, "Keep thy heart with all diligence; for out of it are the issues of life."

The righteousness of Christ is the glorious armor for us to wear in a world of sin. As mentioned before, the righteousness is imputed. Paul said, "For he hath made him to be sin for us, who knew no sin; that we might be made the righteousness of God in him" (2 Corinthians 5:21). It is also practical righteousness.

Paul said, "For the grace of God that bringeth salvation hath appeared to all men, Teaching us that, denying ungodliness and worldly lusts, we should live soberly, righteously, and godly, in this present world" (Titus 2:11-12).

The righteous team must always be **the ready troop**. Paul says, we are to have "our feet shod with the preparation of the gospel of peace" (Ephesians 6:15). The Roman soldier did not wear boots but sandals. These sandals were made with nails that gripped the ground firmly. Other parts of the gear may have been removed to rest while on the battlefield, but the sandals remained on their feet. The sandals were a sign of readiness to march and do battle.

This verse simply means that we must be prepared to go and share the gospel at all times. Jesus said, "Go ye into all the world, and preach the gospel to every creature" (Mark 16:15). Before returning to heaven, He said, "But ye shall receive power, after the Holy Ghost is come upon you: and ye shall be witnesses unto me both in Jerusalem, and in all Judea, and in Samaria, and unto the uttermost part of the earth" (Acts 1:8).

In order for the troops to be ready at all times, **the regiment's training** must be continuous. In all of the branches of the armed forces, you have basic training that takes place after being enlisted. It is exactly what it is called: basic training. After basic training, the soldier moves to another level by training every day while on duty. The training does not stop. You cannot be prepared without regular training taking place. We should study the Scripture and work on methods of soul-winning continuously.

Paul said, "Above all, taking the shield of faith, wherewith ye shall be able to quench all the fiery darts of the wicked" (Ephesians 6:16). The shields of the Roman soldiers were large enough to cover the whole soldier's body. When the soldiers walked side by side, the shields were linked together to form a wall of iron. **The real test** that shows whether or not the Christian soldier will stand is found in this verse. It is all about faith. Think about the importance of faith for a moment. The writer of

Hebrews said, "But without faith it is impossible to please him: for he that cometh to God must believe that he is, and that he is a rewarder of them that diligently seek him" (Hebrews 11:6).

James said, "Count it all joy when ye fall into divers temptations; Knowing this, that the trying of your faith worketh patience" (James 1:2-3). When Jesus prayed for Peter, he said (Luke 22:31-32), "Simon, Simon, behold, Satan hath desired to have you, that he may sift you as wheat: But I have prayed for thee, that thy faith fail not: and when thou are converted, strengthen thy brethren." Before facing Nero's chopping block, Paul said, "I have fought a good fight, I have finished my course, I have kept the faith" (2 Timothy 4:7). As long as we live on this earth, we will always be in the range of the fiery darts aimed in our direction, but the shield of faith will quench them.

Paul said, "And take the helmet of salvation" (Ephesians 6:17a). This valuable piece of armor deals with **the renegade's target**. I mentioned the importance of having the heart protected earlier. Now Paul deals with another vital part of the human anatomy that must be protected, the head. When Paul speaks of the "helmet of salvation," he is picturing the helmet of the Roman soldier worn into the battle. The Roman soldier knew that a blow to the head could be fatal. A serious blow to the head in battle could easily take a soldier out.

With certain wounds to the other parts of the body, the soldier could possibly continue to stand. The right blow to the head could take the soldier down and out. The helmet of salvation helps the believer to stand mentally. Satan attacks our minds. If Satan can convince us that we are not really saved, he has received a victory. You are redeemed. Yet you didn't do anything for it to happen. You were "bought with a price." You received the free gift of salvation. You didn't earn or deserve it. Nothing you do can separate you from the love of God. You are saved forever.

Therefore, we need a spiritual helmet to protect our thoughts from Satan's influence and interference. Satan has been described in the Scripture as "the accuser of the brethren." We cannot fall for this trick of the devil. You do not lose your salvation as a result of committing sins after God has saved you. In 2 Corinthians 10:5, Paul said, "Casting down imaginations, and every high thing that exalteth itself against the knowledge of God, and bringing into captivity every thought to the obedience of Christ."

The helmet of salvation creates **the renewed thoughts** needed for the Christian soldier to fight on the battlefield. This is why you need your thoughts renewed daily. This is what Paul had in mind when he said, "And be not conformed to this world: but be ye transformed by the renewing of your mind, that ye may prove what is that good, and acceptable, and perfect, will of God" (Romans 12:2).

When we think right, we live right. This is what Paul was referring to in Philippians 4:8 when he said, "Finally, brethren, whatsoever things are true, whatsoever things are honest, what-soever things are just, whatsoever things are pure, whatsoever things are lovely, whatsoever things are of good report; if there be any virtue, and if there be any praise, think on these things."

Let's look at the value of **the recorded testaments**. We need the sword of the Spirit, which is the Word of God (see Ephesians 6:17b). Up until this point, all of the armor mentioned dealt with defensive measures only. Paul finally gives us the offensive weapon to use in this battle. We are to use the sword to attack the enemy. It is the recorded testimony known as the Word of God used as our defensive weapon. The principalities, powers, and rulers cannot prevail against the Word of God. In describing the Word of God, the writer of Hebrews said, it is "quick [living], and powerful, and sharper than any two-edged sword" (see Hebrews 4:12).

Did you pay any attention to the fact that **the rear tackle** is missing? Why? The Christian soldier is to face the enemy and not retreat from him. God does not need cowardly soldiers in His army. Instead of running, we should make the enemy retreat. James said, "Submit yourselves therefore to God. Resist the devil, and he will flee from you" (James 4:7). He opens the next verse (James 4:8) saying, "Draw nigh to God, and he will draw nigh to you. . . . " The devil knows he is in trouble if God draws nigh to you.

THE CONCLUDING WORDS

Paul addresses **the serious praying** required of God's soldiers. He says, "Praying always with all prayer and supplication in the Spirit, and watching thereunto with all perseverance and supplication for all saints" (Ephesians 6:18). We fight this battle as serious prayer warriors. It is great to enter the battle fully dressed and armed, but something else is required. It is constant and ceaseless praying. The writer of 1 Chronicles says, "Seek the Lord and his strength, seek his face continually" (1 Chronicles 16:11). In Philippians, Paul says, "Be careful for nothing; but in every thing by prayer and supplication with thanksgiving let your requests be made known unto God" (Philippians 4:6). Satan knows he is in trouble when we spend a lot of time praying.

The word *praying* deals with all aspects of prayer: confession, praise, petition, etc. The word *supplication* deals with **the specific petitions** submitted to the Lord. It is not a general and broad prayer request. It is a petition for a specific personal need. We must learn to be specific when we talk to the Lord and believe God will answer our request. It is worth mentioning that His answer may not always be the response we hoped for but it is always the right response.

Serious praying and specific petitions are worthless without **the Spirit's participation.** His involvement is critical. Praying in the Spirit has nothing to do with shouting, falling out, or speaking ecstatic utterances. He brings to our minds passages of Scripture for us to include in our prayers. He speaks what we cannot speak. In Romans, Paul says, "Likewise the Spirit also helpeth our infirmities: for we know not what we should pray for as we ought: but the Spirit itself maketh intercession for us with groanings, which cannot be uttered. And he that searcheth the hearts knoweth what is the mind of the Spirit, because he maketh intercession for the saints according to the will of God" (Romans 8:26-27).

He lists a few points of emphasis for our prayer lists. We shouldn't be selfish in our petitioning. We should pray for **the saints' perseverance** (see Ephesians 6:18b). On a weekly basis, I receive an email from a local pastor asking me the same question. "How can I pray for you this week?" I always respond with a specific need in my life that I am petitioning God for. This is what Paul is talking about here. We need to pray for the needs of our brothers and sisters in the Lord. Just as I share the prayer request with my friend weekly, I also share my praise reports related to answered prayers.

The next petition deals with **the strengthened preacher**. Paul basically says, "When you pray, please don't forget about me." He said, "And for me, that utterance may be given unto me, that I may open my mouth boldly, to make known the mystery of the gospel. For which I am an ambassador in bonds: that therein I may speak boldly, as I ought to speak" (Ephesians 6:19-20). Earlier, I mentioned the pastor contacting me weekly about my prayer requests. He will tell you that the request he receives most often deals with needing strength for the vocation. This is what Paul had in mind here. He wanted the church to pray for him to have strength and courage to preach the Word of God.

Let's not forget that Paul is chained to a guard, charged with treason, and due to be arraigned before Nero at any moment. He needed the people to pray for him to have holy boldness to keep proclaiming the truth in spite of the obstacles faced. Isn't it interesting that Paul did not request for them to pray that he would be released from prison? I believe Paul realized that he had been commissioned by God to be there and he had a mission to take care of.

Paul said, "That ye also may know my affairs, and how I do, Tychicus, a beloved brother and faithful minister in the Lord, shall make known to you all things: Whom I have sent unto you for the same purpose, that ye might know our affairs, and that he might comfort your hearts" (Ephesians 6:21-22). In these verses, Paul speaks highly of **the sibling present** in his life.

The thought of Paul being in prison grieved the saints in Ephesus. Paul knew the saints in Ephesus were concerned about his welfare and wanted to know how he was doing. He had an eyewitness who could tell them. We are all brothers and sisters in the Lord. We are family. Family is determined by the "blood" connection. Yes, we are blood brothers and sisters as a result of being washed in the blood of the Lamb. Tychicus is described as a "beloved brother." He was a little closer to Paul than the average brother or sister. This meant there was a special bond between them.

Why was there a special bond between them? I think it has something to do with the next descriptive point. Paul addresses **the sacred profession** of Tychicus as well. He is described as a faithful minister of the Lord. The word translated *minister, diakonos,* means "an active servant." The minister should never forget what the word means. Tychicus was entrusted to deliver the letters of Paul to the Ephesians, Colossians, and to Philemon (see Ephesians 6:21-22 and Colossians 4:7-8). He was called a "fellowservant" in Colossians 4:7.

Look at **the salutation proclaimed** at the end of the letter. Paul says, "Peace be to the brethren, and love with faith, from God the Father and the Lord Jesus Christ. Grace be with all them that love our Lord Jesus Christ in sincerity" (Ephesians 6:24). He invokes peace upon them. On the battlefield, it is great to have peace among the rank and file. He invokes love with faith upon them. Love is the source and faith is the force. Finally, he invokes grace upon them. He opened the letter with grace (see Ephesians 1:2) and closes it with grace (see Ephesians 6:24).

We cannot overlook the last word of Ephesians 6:24. Salvation is all about **the sincere practice** and not the sinless performance. The word *sincerity* settles the debate of whether or not a person can lose his salvation. The key is to be sincere with your confession. All believers are still under construction. I, just like you, am a work in progress. I blow it but I sincerely serve Him and repent when I sin. There are people who claim to be saved and they are not sincere. Yes, they come to church but they haven't sincerely surrendered to the Savior.

He closes the letter with **the solemn postlude** used in all of his epistles. He says, "Amen" (Ephesians 6:24b). The word means "may it be so." It deals with the solemn ratification or approval of an expression of faith. What better word to close this powerful, profound, and prolific letter. Let the church say, "Amen!"

CONTACT INFORMATION

To order additional copies of this book, please visit
www.redemption-press.com.
Also available on Amazon.com and BarnesandNoble.com
Or by calling toll free 1-844-2REDEEM.

Also the book can be obtained from:
Antioch Fellowship Missionary Baptist Church
www.afmbc.org

CPSIA information can be obtained
at www.ICGtesting.com
Printed in the USA
LVHW020408031120
670552LV00012B/219

9 781683 140221